MW00882745

UP THE ALLEY AND OVER THE FENCE

Memoirs of a Chicago Boyhood, 1930 - 1951,

From the Great Depression Through

World War II

By Walter Oleksy

Waltmax69@gmail.com

Order book from CreateSpace eStore

CONTENTS

Introduction

Listen, my children, and you shall hear
Of the midnight ride of a can of beer.
Up the alley and over the fence
I've got the can,
Who's got ten cents?
-- The Midnight Ride of a Can of Beer

My sister Mary Jane, at the age of seven, was a professional mourner. This was back in 1936 when we lived on the South Side of Chicago. Rain, snow, or sunshine, Sis went to one of the neighborhood funeral parlors and stood out front. Lanky and with long dark hair, clutching a prayer book or string of Rosary beads, she bowed her head and sobbed. For this she was rewarded with pennies from the bereaved who came to pay their last respects to the deceased.

We were Catholic and Democrats, but Sis was the first real liberal I knew. She never knew the religion, occupation, or anything else about the person lying in their casket inside the chapel.

Sis only got a hint as to who they were in life because of the color ribbon on the crepe, the white wicker basket of fresh-cut flowers that stood outside the chapel door. A light purple ribbon was for a man, white for a woman, pink for a baby or child, and silver for an elderly man or woman. Years later, purple became the standard color ribbon for anyone deceased.

It didn't matter to Mary Jane who was in their box inside the chapel. They deserved the best cry she could send them off with for a penny.

During the school year, Sis had great hours. She only worked Saturday mornings. When school was out for summer vacation, she made the rounds of the chapels almost every day.

If she needed pennies in a hurry, she skipped the other funeral parlors and took up work outside the Jewish. She found that, for some reason, the Jewish bereaved gave her more pennies than Catholics or Protestants.

Sis taught me resourcefulness and helped me learn how to survive in hard times. Eighty-three years later, after beating cancer, she's still teaching me that important lesson of life.

A year and a half younger than my sister, my job was to go around our block to aunts or neighbors and ask for their empty soda or milk bottles. We and our older brother Johnny Boy took them to the grocery store and redeemed them for their deposits of one or two cents each.

When we pooled our pennies, we earned enough for show money. It only cost a dime to go to a neighborhood movie palace and see two features straight from their run in the downtown theaters. Maybe an Errol Flynn adventure or a Sonja Henie ice-skating musical. Or we went to a second-run theater and saw three movies a few years old, for only a nickel. There we saw a John Wayne or Buck Jones western, maybe a Johnny Weissmuller "Tarzan," and a Bela Lugosi "spooky."

Johnny Boy's job was to take all three of us to the movies, stopping in the five-and-ten-cent store on the way to buy a pound of licorice or butter kisses for a dime. Then we entered the dark world of the movie house and sat with our legs curled up under us. We didn't take our eyes off the screen for four or six hours while Johnny Boy divided up the candy from a big bag. He sat between us and doled out the goodies: One butter kiss for Mary, one for me.

There in the dark, was that when I began not to trust my big brother? I was sure he took two for himself every time.

*****

Millions of people lost their jobs when I was a boy growing up in Chicago during The Great Depression of the 1930s. People survived the hard times by their resourcefullness and sheer determination not to cave in under adversity. Today, in times of recession and job-loss, many people are faced with the same challenges we were over half a century ago. But we made it and, if they keep at it and never give up faith or trying, they can, too.

My sister's and brother's grandchildren have a much easier life than we did. To them, the 1930s and 1940s are ancient history, somewhere after the Ice Age and before rock and roll and the invention of television. Our trials in those distant years are foreign but somewhat curious to them, and they've asked many times, "Tell what it was like, when you were a kid?"

To answer them, and to tell a story of our survival, I decided to write about my boyhood, my mother and father, and sister and brother in the "good old days" when we were young.

You might ask, who cares? My folks and nobody else in the family ever became famous or even infamous for anything. They just got born, worked usually not at what they did best but what they could earn a living at, got married or stayed single, had kids or didn't, lived ordinary lives and sometimes did stupid things before they died and left almost no footprints in the sand but often imprints in our hearts.

No, they weren't very important. The thing is, you'll probably see yourself in them or us, and others you know as well.

The book's title refers to an old beer-drinking song my father and his brothers and sisters used to sing after week-end poker parties at Grandma's house on the South Side of Chicago before World War II:

"Up the alley and over the fence. I've got the can. Who's got ten cents?"

In the 1930s, you could take a tin pail to the corner tavern and get it filled with tap beer for a dime. For the children, a pail or pitcher of root beer also only cost ten cents.

You can't buy much for a dime today. Back then, people sat on their front porches or door steps on summer nights and talked while they drank their beer, and maybe listened to someone up the block pedal their feet on a player piano.

Speaking of porches reminds me, we never locked our doors and if anyone had a car, which we didn't, they never locked it for fear it would be stolen. On hot summer nights, with no air-conditioning and maybe just one electric fan for the whole house, my sister and brother and I would drag our mattresses onto the second or third floor back porch of whatever old building we were living in and sleep there. Our folks and we kids never worried that anyone would come in from the alley and strangle, rape, or kidnap us.

There was no drug problem back in the 1930s, to cause people to rob, steal, or kill anyone for a few dollars. The only "dope" we kids knew about was if one of our playmates was maybe a little "off," or as I just heard, "They're one sandwich short of a picnic."

They say we can learn a lot from history, if we take the time to read it, so maybe we don't make the same mistakes twice. I believe that's true. I also tend to believe it's true about a person's family history.

Children today hardly get to know their parents before the mother and father divorce. It's too bad, because everything else aside, it's important to know who your folks are, or were. It helps a person when they grow up, to get to know who *they* are.

Most of the people in the stories that follow have gone to that big poker game in the sky. You probably know or miss people like them.

Anyway, these are the stories I tell when the new generation in the family ask, "Tell what it was like, when you were a kid?"

This book is kind of a confession and I'm going to do my best to be honest about myself but, of course, I'm not going to tell you *everything*. As Holden Caulfield said in *Catcher in the Rye*, the rest of the family would have two hemorrhages apiece if I told anything too personal about them. And I sure hope they don't let a new book get published that tells about Holden as a senior citizen. J.D. Salinger had that in the courts and won.

Chapter One

Chicago, Chicago, that toddlin' town

In case you aren't from Chicago or don't know that much about it, here's my amateur historian's version of the highlights of its history. I think it's important to know something about the city I grew up in, so you can fit me into it over the twenty years of my boyhood, because when you come down to it, my story is as much about Chicago as it is about me.

Poet Carl Sandburg called Chicago "the city of big shoulders" because he likened it to a big, strapping, hard-working young man whose shoulders one could lean on.

He also called Chicago "the hog butcher for the world," because as the nation's central railroad terminus, much of the country's livestock was shipped to the city's Stock Yards to be processed.

Chicago got its nickname as the "windy city" not because of its strong breezes but because New York newspaper editor Charles A. Dana didn't believe Chicago could build a world's fair and wrote in 1892, "Don't pay any attention to the nonsensical claims of that windy city." But the city did get and build a fabulous world's fair, the World's Columbian Exposition of 1893-94.

One of the architects of the fair was Louis Sullivan, who together with D.H. Burnham, Frank Lloyd Wright, and others some years later made Chicago a leading architectural center.

The world's first steel-frame skyscraper, the ten-story Home Insurance Company building, was built in Chicago in 1885 by architect William Le Baron Jenney. He reportedly got the idea years earlier while visiting the Philippines where he saw houses balanced on bamboo struts. Afterwards he worked on his skyscraper idea when helping to build latticed iron railroad-type bridges for General William Sherman's army during the Civil War. Jenney's skyscraper paved the way for large-scale urban development.

Chicago hosted a second world's fair in 1933-34 when despite a deepening depression, the city celebrated its 100th anniversary with the Century of Progress. Exhibits previewed the technological wonders of the future but perhaps the fair's most popular attraction was fan-dancer Sally Rand and her "Little Egypt" show.

My feeling for Chicago goes back to its beginnings and first settlers, the tribes of the Algonquin Indian nation.

Chicago began as a swamp where Indians gave it the name *chi-kaug-ong,* which meant wild onion, because the smelly plants grew in profusion along the river at the Southwest foot of Lake Michigan.

From its discovery by the French Jesuit missionary Jacques Marquette and explorer Louis Jolliet in 1673 until 1763, the area had been under French rule. After the French and Indian War in that year, it came under the British flag and remained so until the end of the Revolutionary War. The British then ceded the Western Territories to the Americans at the treaty of peace in 1783.

Pottawatomie and other Indian tribes continued to live and hunt in the area, pushed there by the continuous Westward expansion of American pioneers. After their defeat in 1794 at the Battle of Fallen Timbers in Northeast Ohio, the Indians' days of freedom in the region were virtually over. General "Mad" Anthony Wayne's victory all but secured the Northwest frontier for white settlers.

At the Treaty of Greenville, "one piece of land six miles square, at the mouth of the Chicago River, emptying into the Southwest end of Lake Michigan" was granted to the United States for use as a portage, allowing a fort to be built there. Settlers were encouraged to move further Westward and into the region at the foot of Lake Michigan.

A fort was built there in 1803 by soldiers sent from Detroit, not only to protect settlers but to safeguard American traders who were encroaching upon the privileges of the British. The British had for years won the favor of area Indians by trading them guns, ammunition, and whiskey for their fur pelts.

The fort was named after General Henry Dearborn, then Secretary of War. Forest stood nearby on the North side of the river and a few trees dotted the South branch of the river, beyond which was mainly open prairie. The Grand Prairie extended for hundreds of miles Westward.

Tecumseh, one of the great Indian chiefs, tried to unite the tribes of the area into an Indian Confederacy, to reclaim their lost land and drive the settlers away. When war broke out again between the Americans and British in 1812, Tecumseh sided with the redcoats. When the fort was ordered evacuated, warriors from many of the local tribes attacked the soldiers and settlers as they began their retreat to Fort Wayne, Indiana. In a bloody raid along the lakefront, more than half of about a hundred soldiers and civilians including nearly a dozen children were killed in what became known as The Fort Dearborn Massacre.

I've always been fascinated by that bloody battle and in fact believe I was in it, in an earlier life, not to take anything away from Shirley MacLaine who says we've all lived dozens of other lives before the one we're living now. But as far back as grammar school, I've read everything I could find about the Fort Dearborn Massacre, then written term papers and articles about it, and believe I was either a soldier or militiaman during the terrible battle. I feel as if I was there, but am not so sure whether I kept my scalp.

After the War of 1812, the tribes regained control of the area but by 1830 several dozen settlers returned to the lakefront and began putting up houses. On August 12, 1833, Chicago was incorporated as a village. The following month a treaty was signed with the Pottawatomie, Chippewa, Ottawa and Kickapoo Indians of the region and they agreed to give up Illinois and move West to the Mississippi River.

Chicago began growing fast after that and by 1848 the population was slightly over 20,000. The city's claim as a railroad hub began in 1854 when the Rock Island Railroad connected Chicago to Lockport and the Mississippi River.

In 1865, the Union Stock Yards opened on the Southwest Side and the city began its fame as a meat processor. Five years later a census revealed Chicago had 1,481 saloons and 1,065 groceries, testimony that Man can not live by bread alone.

Today it's considered a fairy tale, but a cow that kicked over a lantern was blamed for the Chicago Fire on Oct. 8, 1871 that took 300 lives and destroyed 18,000 mostly wooden homes and other buildings. Within a few years, Chicago was rebuilt as a city of stone and steel.

As part of the rebuilding, the huge iron and steel interstate Industrial Exposition Building was erected in 1873, making Chicago a convention capital.

Besides the skyscraper, Chicago is known for some other "firsts" of varying degrees of importance.

Abner Doubleday is credited with inventing baseball in 1839 in Cooperstown, New York, but fifty years later, some young football fans at Chicago's Farragut Boat Club invented softball.

The world's first sextuplets were delivered to the Bushnell family of Chicago in September, 1866.

Dr. John Dill Robertson became Chicago's health commissioner that same year, the first man in history to be so appointed on the strength of his claim that bathing caused diseases. He said he was in fine health and hadn't bathed in two years.

The first accurate adding machine came out of Chicago in 1887. The zipper was invented by a Chicagoan, Whitcomb L. Judson. In 1891 he put together a linkage of hooks and eyes with a sliding clasp, calling it a "locker and unlocker of shoes."

The world's first successful human heart operation was performed in Chicago in 1893 after a man was stabbed in the chest during a saloon brawl. He was taken to a hospital where a black surgeon, Daniel Hale Williams, tied off a severed artery and sewed the edges of the man's heart sac together. The man lived another twenty years but Williams died in relative obscurity at the age of 73 in the early 1930s.

Also in 1893, the world's first Ferris wheel, 260 feet tall, was built for Chicago's Columbian Exposition by George Ferris, a civil engineer. The world's first cafeteria opened in Chicago in 1895.

In 1899 Chicago opened the nation's first Juvenile Court. A year later it became the first city to reverse the flow of a major river, causing the Chicago River to flow "uphill" and turning it back onto its source in order to carry sewage away from Lake Michigan. Engineers did this by closing the river's entrance to the lake and pumping water back through a new drainage canal.

The first American citizen to become a saint, Mother Frances Xavier Cabrini, established hospitals, nurseries, orphanages, and schools in Chicago and New York City during the early part of the century.

Jane Addams founded Hull House in Chicago, one of the first social settlements for the poor in the United States, and in 1931 became the first woman to win the Nobel Peace Prize.

Chicago became one of the nation's great "melting pot" cities in the early 1900s as industries sprang up and jobs attracted thousands of immigrants. Those who came to work and live in Chicago were Germans, Austrians including my mother and her parents, Poles such as my paternal grand-father and his people, Czechs, Lithuanians, Croats, Italians, Greeks, Scandinavians, Irish, Jews, Chinese, American Negroes, and in more recent years, Hispanics.

The world's first truly efficient drawbridge was the double-leaf trunnion bascule "Chicago-style" bridge, built in 1902.

The Volstead Act in 1919 making it a crime to sell or buy beer, wine, or hard liquor began another kind of "first" for Chicago. Throughout the 1920s and even long after the unpopular law's repeal in 1933, Chicago became the nation's most notorious battleground for gangster warfare as Al Capone and other rival mobsters competed for control of the liquor business in various parts of the city and suburbs.

The first pinball machines were invented by a Chicago game manufacturer in 1931, called Ballyhoo, a coin-operated game two feet long and eighteen inches wide. Beer sold in cans was introduced in Chicago in 1935, selling 160 million cans the first year.

On December 2, 1942, one of the most significant events in World War II took place at the University of Chicago when a group of scientists working on the government's secret atomic bomb project achieved the world's first nuclear chain reaction, ushering in the Atomic Age.

A hard act to follow, a few years later Chicago restaurateur Ric Riccardo introduced the nation to deep-dish pizza, importing the recipe from Italy. And in 1951, Chicagoans participated in the first pay-television experiment.

Chicago also is the birthplace of the coeducational public school system, the railroad sleeping car, bifocal contact lens, winding watch, Butterfinger and Baby Ruth candy bars, the bowling tournament, shrimp de jonghe, a comprehensive underground grid-pattern sewage system, the vacuum cleaner, Cracker Jack, Schwinn bicycle, and the suit that comes with two pair of pants.

Billy Sunday, mentioned in the lyrics to Chicago's theme song, was a professional baseball player who turned evangelist. In the late 1890s he held fire-and-brimstone revivals calling for the city's saloons and houses of pleasure to be shut down. He wasn't the last who failed at that.

Chicago was ward politics, one of the world's best French Impressionist art collections in the Art Institute, an elevated system circling the downtown called the "Loop," an intricate subway system, gangsters and cops on-the-take, famous zoo gorillas, one of the most beautiful skylines and lakefronts in the world, holy water and bootleg gin, union battles and crippling strikes, a galaxy of neighborhood restaurants serving delicious ethnic foods, nuns and showgirls, ghettoes and estates, flophouses and mansions, sometimes world-beating baseball, football, and basketball teams, iron-willed mayors at least one of whom was a President-maker (Richard J. Daley supporting John F. Kennedy), movie theaters every few blocks, a tavern on almost every street corner, unemployed men selling apples, tea parlors and speakeasies, jazz joints and one of the great symphony orchestras, Polish sausage and Communion wafers, sweating in the summer and freezing in the winter, church bells and blaring police and fire sirens, and machinegun bullets.

The Chicago I was born into was or would be all that and more.

Chapter Two

Back home again in Indiana

My father must have been a lot like me, because one summer day when he was just a little boy living in Indiana farm country, he watched as one of his aunts picked potato bugs off the plants.

"Don't pick too many of them," he cautioned her. "I don't think my Mommy and I are gonna like 'em."

Dad always knew a good thing, or bad, when he saw one.

My father was born in Anderson, Indiana, and my mother in Landeck, Austria. This is how they met and married and had three adorable children, one of whom is me.

A little northeast of Indianapolis, Anderson is a small city on the White River, not the banks of the Wabash. The closest anyone from there ever came to becoming famous was the poet James Whitcomb Riley who wrote a weekly column for the old *Anderson Democrat* in 1877, and Carl Erskine who pitched for the Brooklyn Dodgers in the 1950s.

Dad's father had come to this country in about 1910 from the Ukraine which then belonged to Poland. It later became part of the Soviet Union and in 1991 regained its independence. Many Poles emigrated to America early in this century and settled in Indiana. George Oleksy joined them and put down new roots in Anderson. Soon after, he married a sturdy woman also of Polish descent named Kate who began having a large family, starting with my father.

The offspring grew to number ten and the family lived in an old frame house in the Polish section of town called "The Acre." Bedrooms kept getting added on as more of John's brothers and sisters were born.

In 1964, when the population was 67,500, someone said "Anderson is a monument to indifference." I don't know if it still is, or was when my father's side of our family lived there, but it couldn't have been very exciting. It became pretty much a one industry town, producing Delco-Remy car batteries.

When he was sixteen in 1917, John's passion and main pursuit when he wasn't working with the rest of the family in a neighborhood factory where they made metal files, was playing baseball. When he and his brothers weren't getting in fights with the Irish who lived across from The Acre. They were usually harmless fist-fights that evolved out of disagreements over foul balls or home runs.

When John was barely out of his teens, he'd become one of the best and busiest pitchers around and a scout from the Chicago White Sox took an interest in him. But because he played ball too often and hadn't been properly coached, he threw his pitching arm out and never got a chance to play pro ball.

Throughout his life, my father never got the break he needed. He was always on the bench, never back in the game so he could hit the big home run that was in him.

The bad right arm kept him off the   diamonds so he got into another sport -- boxing. His friend Jack Lavergne, in his late teens, was a pretty good fighter and Dad and another friend, Buck Genda, became Jack's corner handlers. Jack was an up-and-coming club fighter in the state when one day his career ended abruptly.

It hadn't been his friends' fault, but Jack's manager signed him up for too many fights with not enough rest time in between. One night, Jack was getting the better of another man in the ring, when the bell clanged ending a round. He went to his corner to sit on his stool and get some advice from his trainer while his friends toweled him off. Joe noticed something that scared him. Jack had become punchy.

The fight was over for Jack. He never fought again and wasn't much for any kind of work after that.

Pro baseball was over for John before it could begin, so he became a spectator in the sport he loved so much. He and his brothers and sisters began going to see the White Sox games in Chicago. The biggest game, they missed.

In 1919, when John was 18, the White Sox lost the World Series to Cincinnati and it turned out that two years later Sox pitcher Bill Burns admitted that the Sox players had fixed the game.

It was a blow to baseball fans everywhere, but nowhere as much as on The Acre in Anderson. Only the good news that year of the Boston Red Sox's Babe Ruth setting a new home-run record for a season, twenty-nine, made the sandlot players in Indiana feel better.

After those visits to see the White Sox play in Comiskey Park in Chicago, John and his brothers and sisters went out to one of the South Side ballrooms, the Trianon or the White City amusement park, and picked up dance partners. Their favorite bands were those of Eddy Howard and Wayne King.

One night at the Trianon John was about 24, a handsome dark-haired, strapping six foot four inch, 200-plus pounds, when he saw a real looker waiting to be asked to dance. She was medium-tall and medium-built, with wavy black hair in the popular boyish bobbed style of the day. Prettier than any girl he'd ever seen.

Maybe what he liked best about the young woman who was about eighteen was how much she enjoyed herself. He'd never seen anyone love to dance as much as this girl did. Even though he didn't care much at all for dancing, he knew it was how a young man could meet a young lady, so he asked her for a turn around the dance floor.

She liked his masculine good looks and polite manner and helped him with his awkward footwork. Later, after a swell evening together, he drove her home. He thought she was the cat's meow. She thought he was keen, too.

The only thing was, he lived out of the state and she lived in Chicago. Her name was Pauline and she came from a large Austrian family that lived on the North Side of the city. In fact, she had come with her parents in steerage class from Austria by ocean liner only about ten years before.

There was only one thing for Pauline to do. She went after John. On weekends when he came to see the Sox play, they met at the Trianon. When he couldn't come to Chicago, she took the train and went to see him in Anderson.

Kate didn't like Pauline. She was too peppy. Too much a Flapper. John's mother had picked out another future bride for her eldest son, the first who would marry and leave home. Agnes was a nice enough girl, but John had fallen hard for the Twinkle-toes of the Trianon.

George's and Kate's family grew to include five more sons and four daughters. One of the girls, Mamie, died of diphtheria in Anderson at the age of eleven, while another, Theresa, was to die after the family moved to Chicago. She was waked at home and it was probably her ghost who haunted her funeral, which I'll tell about a little later.

In 1925, the autumn of the year John and Pauline met, George and Kate moved the family from Anderson to the South Side of Chicago. They bought a brick bungalow in the 5200 block of South Peoria Street. George became a janitor for some nearby apartment buildings and Kate took in laundry. Moving to Chicago removed one important obstacle to John and Pauline getting engaged. Agnes got left behind.

The geographic problem of their courtship was solved, but Kate still didn't approve of Pauline. The Flapper was too interested in dancing to be a good wife to Kate's son. Besides, she'd chased after him.

But Pauline was as good and hard-working as a girl could be, working as a telephone operator for Illinois Bell in Chicago. And besides, it was Prohibition and Kate was making home brew hooch in the bathtub. How good was Kate, anyway?

One night at the house on Peoria Street, Pauline had it. She would make a little whoopee. When Kate was away in the parlor, Pauline sat on the kitchen table. Lifting her skirt to the knee to expose a little rolled down silk stocking, she then lit up a cigarette, though she had never smoked before. If she was going to be accused of being a fast woman, she might as well be one, if only for a joke.

Wouldn't you know Kate took that moment to come into the kitchen. When she saw Pauline she nearly had a heart attack. No woman like that would ever marry a son of hers!

The wedding took place several months later and, afterward, John and Pauline moved into the apartment upstairs from his parents. Kate maintained her dislike of Pauline until their relations became so strained, not long after the birth of her first child, named John, Jr., that Pauline left and took the baby with her. If John loved her enough, he would leave his mother's house and join his wife and son.

John did and he and Pauline rented an apartment which brought, finally, some peace to the woman who a few years later would be my mother. George, by the way, liked Pauline right away, but his voice and vote never counted much against Kate's. She was bigger than him.

One weekend when John, Jr. was just a baby, the proud young parents decided to visit some old friends in Anderson and show him off. Pauline had spent months hand-sewing some beautiful baby outfits for him, including a blue velveteen Little Lord Fauntleroy suit.

All was packed into some suitcases together with changes of clothes for them that weekend. They didn't have a car of their own, so they drove down to Anderson with some friends in their touring car. It didn't have a trunk, so all the suitcases were tied on to the running boards.

The job of watching the suitcases was put in the care of one of John's friends. The only problem with that was, the young man only had one good eye. Somewhere along the way, the suitcases fell off the car. They weren't noticed missing until the friends reached Anderson.

It didn't make sense to try to retrace their route and find the lost luggage. They gave up that idea and began driving to the home of their friend in Anderson, Pearl White.

When they reached the row of identical houses on her block, they rang her bell but there was no answer. After several more rings with no response, John tried the knob and found that the front door was open.

"Let's go in and get the party started," he said. Pearl was probably out buying some ice for their drinks and would be back any minute.

Everyone got busy. Some of Kate's bathtub gin was poured into tall glasses, furniture was moved out of the parlor, and the carpet was rolled up. Someone sat down at the piano and began to play some of the hit songs of the 1926-1927 era -- "Bye Bye Blackbird," "Blue Skies," "Shaking the Blues Away," and "The Best Things in Life Are Free." The Flappers and their partners were doing the Charleston and the Varsity Drag.

After about an hour, a woman they didn't know came into the parlor and asked what all the strangers were doing there.

"Who are *you* ?" John inquired.

"Where's Pearl?" Pauline asked.

The woman's eyes widened. "Pearl White? Oh, she lives two houses down!"

Practicing the good neighbor policy, the woman went up the block and got Pearl. The party stayed where it started.

Two years after John, Jr., Pauline was expecting again, in the coldest January in years and at the start of a big snowstorm.

John still had no car, and there was no telephone in the apartment. But Pauline had to get to the hospital somehow because she was going to deliver her child any moment. John ran frantically out into the snowy street in his shirtsleeves, calling for help. But no motorist stopped.

Finally, a police car drove up. Two Irish cops got out and one asked, "What's all the fuss about?" John was too excited to explain, so they followed the anxious young man up to the apartment on the second floor and looked in. When they saw it was just a woman going to have a baby, they left laughing and were no help at all.

Giving up, the anxious father-to-be found a phone and called the doctor, but he wasn't in. Next, John did the only thing he could think of. He called his mother. Kate earned money as a midwife, but lived too far away to come over in the emergency.

"Looks like *you'll* have to deliver the baby," she told her son.

Over his protests, Kate gave John instructions on the phone. Afterward, he went back home to play midwife himself.

Pauline was scared, but trusting. During difficult labor and the delivery, she kept her eyes on a framed painting of the Blessed Virgin on one bedroom wall. While Joe tried to remember Kate's instructions, the expectant mother prayed to the Virgin to help her and her child.

After the little girl was born, John nervously cut the umbilical cord with a pair of scissors from his wife's sewing basket. Pauline named the baby Mary, in honor of the Mother of Jesus.

A few hours later, the doctor showed up. "I couldn't have done a better job," he told the new father, patting him on the back.

Mary soon became known as Mary Jane and, a year and a half after my sister was born, I came into the world on a hot June night and was named Walter after a Godfather uncle I never laid eyes on after the christening. My mother's older sister, also named Mary, became my Godmother and favorite aunt.

Only about four months after I was born, my mother was pregnant again, but didn't know it. She was standing on a chair, hanging curtains, when she became dizzy and fell. The twin boys who would have become my kid brothers died, one a day apart from the other.

That was 1930 and hard times were ahead. Wall Street had laid an egg the year before and The Great Depression had begun.

Hard times were ahead for me, too. I never got the younger brother I would grow up wanting.

Chapter Three

Edelweiss, edelweiss,
every morning you greet me

The frail old woman was bent over high up on the Austrian mountainside cutting hay with a sickle in the blazing August sun.

"Aren't you tired?" I asked in what little German I knew from college.

She straightened and smiled. Holding the sickle in her left hand, she extended her right arm to take in the majestic vista of mountains, valleys, sun-filled sky and clouds, and replied, "Would you be tired, working out here?"

It was 1957 and I was in the army in Germany, on leave to visit the village my mother was born in. When people laugh at me for loving "The Sound of Music" because they say the movie is too "schmaltzy," I tell them that story.

Landeck, near Innsbruck, is a pastoral village of narrow cobblestone streets and old wooden gingerbread houses with red geraniums in their window boxes, situated in a valley along the Inn River deep in the Arlberg Alps. One of my greatest joys there was hiking up into the mountains to pick edelweiss, the little white snow flower.

The village of my mother's birth in 1907 lies on one side of the river, and a stone fortress like castle is built into the mountainside on the other. Villagers farm the meadows and mountainsides or raise cattle and sheep. In the evening they gather at the hotel's garden cafe and eat wiener schnitzel and drink dark beer while listening to a musician play Johann Strauss waltzes on the zither.

To some, that may be schmaltzy. To me, it's heaven. What the world needs now, to paraphrase the song of a few years ago, is less noise and violence and more schmaltz. There are a lot of worse things to overdose from.

Pauline's father was the village cobbler. Max not only repaired shoes but made them, especially for the local prince and his family. Being a respected artisan of the community, he was allowed to wear fur on the collar of his winter coat. In Landeck, that was the highest mark of distinction a man could achieve this side of nobility. It didn't make Max rich, but it did make him proud.

Max married a strong, healthy girl from his village named Maria and, before long, they had two daughters and a son. As children, Pauline, later to be my mother, and her older sister Mary and younger brother Martin lived with their parents in a big old house with a barn underneath it, built into a hill in the center of the village. At dusk, the children helped round up the chickens and livestock and led them into the barn which held the spicy aroma of smoked sausage and bacon.

In 1910, when Pauline was three years old, her father had a falling out with his older brother after their father died. Everything had been left to the older brother. Max saw no future for him in Landeck so he sold the house, left some of the money in the local bank, and put the family on a boat. They came to America to what they hoped would be a better life. Sadly, they met only misfortune.

The family settled in Chicago but did not fare well. Max was reduced from making shoes to repairing them, working ten and twelve hours a day for another shoemaker. Besides not earning much money, he began to grow ill from the glue used in repairing shoes. Meanwhile, Maria grew homesick for her homeland.

Pauline was only about five, in 1912, when her mother decided the family should go back to Austria to live. Her father wanted to stay in Chicago and so did her older sister who was about eight and didn't want to leave the school she liked. Learning about their impending departure, Mary ran away from home and hid under a table at a girlfriend's house. But she was found and went back to Austria with her mother, sister and brother, while Max remained behind in Chicago.

The family only stayed in Austria about a year and a half. By the summer of 1914, war had broken out in Europe. It would be safer back in Chicago, Maria decided. The Austrian government took everyone's savings from the bank but there was enough money left to book second-class passage back to America. By some mistake, they were put in third-class steerage and it was a difficult crossing in the hold of the ship.

Late that summer the family was reunited in Chicago where they rented an apartment on the North Side. In the next few years were born another daughter, Julia, and two more sons, Albert and Louis.

Max continued working as a shoe repairman until his death from illness and an accident after about ten years in this country. Maria was widowed at about the age of forty with no money and six children to support. She began taking in laundry and doing housekeeping, to earn the rent and their food.

There wasn't enough money for any of the children to go to high school, so they had to get the best jobs they could with only a grammar school education. In those years, many boys and girls started their work life at the age of thirteen or fourteen.

Pauline was about twelve in 1919 and too young to work, but her sister was sixteen and got a job away from home. Mary became nursemaid to the little boy and girl of a lawyer and his wife, earning $2 a week plus room and board at their house. After two years she married, then found work as a telephone operator for Illinois Bell.

Too young for other work, Pauline and Julia lived with other families and became children's companions. The wife of the family Pauline lived with loved her and wanted to adopt her, but the husband tried to force his attentions on Pauline and she ran away, back to her mother.

Within the next few years, all three of Pauline's' brothers, who had been sent to different orphanages, died from illness or accidents while in their late teens.

When Pauline turned fourteen she began doing domestic work in the homes of neighborhood families. The following year she found work as a waitress at a hospital, serving the doctors and nurses in their dining room.

While still fifteen, she went to work as housekeeper and baby-sitter for another family when she became ill. A diphtheria epidemic was sweeping the city and her employers thought she had caught it and was a carrier of the disease.

Isolated from the rest of the family she lived with, she was locked in a basement room with iron bars on the windows. Somehow she found paper and pencil and threw a note out that read, "Help me. I'm held prisoner!" No one found the note but, fortunately, the epidemic ended a few days later and she was released, then ran home again to her mother.

After her sixteenth birthday, Pauline lost no time seeking a better job and also became a telephone operator for Illinois Bell. There had not been much fun in her life up to then, so it was no wonder she wanted to find some and began going to Chicago's lively ballrooms on Saturday nights.

She and her sister or some girlfriends from the phone company went to them all... the Aragon, Merry Gardens, Rainbow Gardens, the Edgewater Beach Hotel, White City, Dreamland, Navy Pier. Pauline's favorite haunt became the Trianon on the South Side, because of a handsome young gentleman she met there who lived in Indiana. Even if he did have two left feet.

Chapter Four

Let the rest of the world go by

John and Pauline were married in May, 1926, when he was 26 and she was 19. They honeymooned in Springfield, Illinois, where Pauline's younger sister Julia had gone to live after marrying a coal miner from there when she was sixteen. She had met Frank at a dance at Fort Sheridan north of Chicago shortly after he returned from the Great War.

Most of the wedding party and many other friends and relatives piled into dozens of cars and followed the bride and groom's car halfway to Springfield, honking their horns. Then they turned back to Chicago to celebrate some more.

The honeymoon was the best time Pauline ever had, and she hated to have it end. She had been working as a telephone operator for Illinois Bell and when her week's vacation was up, she neglected to call in to ask for a few more days off, so she lost her job. So had her sister Mary. A hearing problem brought an early end to her career as a telephone operator and she reluctantly went back to being nursemaid for other people's children.

When they returned to Chicago after their extended honeymoon, John got work in a garage as an auto mechanic and Pauline took whatever work she could find. Their first apartment was on Diversey Avenue on Chicago's North Side, then they moved to another on Lincoln Avenue. It was only a few blocks from the Biograph Theater where Public Enemy No. 1 John Dillinger would be gunned down by F.B.I. agents just a few years later.

The family lived in the Lincoln Avenue apartment when I was born in County hospital. I got in its maternity ward with pull. Alice White from Anderson had married a man named Jack and he worked in the *Chicago Tribune* pressroom. Through his connections, Mom gave birth to me in a hospital bed instead of another birthing adventure at home. Dad must have had his fill of midwifery.

About this time, my mother's mother died. After the funeral, a wake was held at my parents' apartment. My mother had a hard time appreciating the way my father's Polish family observed wakes. To her, they were more like drinking parties because all my father's brothers and friends showed up with bottles of bootleg gin or whiskey, since it was still Prohibition. The Volstead Act lasted from 1919 to 1933 and between those years, making or drinking alcohol was a federal crime.

To my father's and everyone's horror at her mother's wake, Mom uncorked all the booze bottles and poured the precious liquid down the toilet, declaring:

"No one's going to get drunk at *my* mother's funeral!"

After the wake that night and my father had fallen asleep, my mother lie in bed awake when an icy hand stroked her forehead. For days afterward, after my father left for work in the morning, my mother looked out the window and saw a woman dressed in black, standing on the street corner. She thought she recognized the woman as her mother. Each day she rushed out of the apartment and started to walk toward her, but the woman would vanish. My mother talked my father into moving shortly after that and never again encountered what she believed to be her mother's ghost.

The hard years began the autumn of the year my sister was born, starting with the stock market crash in October, 1929. The decade of the rich getting richer and the rest of the population sitting atop flagpoles, swallowing goldfish, and dancing until dawn came to a grim end when soon one third of a nation lost their jobs. Among them were my mother and father.

Herbert Hoover, the Republican "prosperity President" who had promised everyone "a chicken in every pot and a car in every garage" in 1928, hadn't made good. In their place all over the country sprung up "Hoovervilles," shantytowns made of cardboard and scrap tin where the unemployed found some shelter from the elements and despair. On Chicago street-corners, men and women sold government surplus apples for five cents apiece.

In 1932, Democrat Franklin Delano Roosevelt was elected President and pledged "a new deal for the American people." At his inaugural the following March he said, "The only thing we have to fear is fear itself -- nameless, unreasoning, unjustified terror."

If you've never been out of work, had little or no hope of getting a job, and not had a dime to your name, with a wife and three children to provide for, you never felt what my father did during those years of the Great Depression. He hadn't lost anything when the banks failed, because he hadn't had any money in them. But he just couldn't find work.

The Century of Progress, Chicago's World's Fair of technological achievement, opened in 1933 and helped a little to take our minds off our empty stomachs. My earliest recollection of being on this planet was being taken there for an afternoon. The thing I remember best is riding in one of the open fair buses with the striped canopies. Maybe that's because my Godmother, Aunt Mary, bought me a Tootsie Toy replica of one.

What meant more to the grown-ups was the repeal of the Volstead act that December and Prohibition ended.

The following year, on July 22, 1934, a month after my fourth birthday, John Dillinger was shot down just a few blocks from where I was playing in a sandbox. The nation's most notorious bank robber and the first gangster on J. Edgar Hoover's most-wanted list was watching a Clark Gable crime movie at the Biograph theater.

One of Dillinger's girlfriends, called "The Lady in Red" because she wore a red dress that hot summer night, had tipped off the F.B.I. that she would be there with him seeing "Manhattan Melodrama." After seeing the movie starring Clark Gable and William Powell as best friends from opposite sides of the law, Dillinger was leaving the theater when twenty G-men gunned him down. A few weeks after his death, my brother took me to see where it happened.

Another of my earliest memories is of seeing with my own eyes the bullet holes in the brickwork of the outside of the theater and the lamp post that had taken some of the hail of shells fired at the gangster. It gave me some idea of how wild Chicago and the nation was when I was four years old. Bonnie and Clyde had met a similar end in Louisiana just three months earlier.

Like it or not, I became a part of that gangster legacy. Ever after, whenever anyone asked me where I was from and I said Chicago, they made a gun of their thumb and index finger, pointed it in my ribs, and gave out with a rhubarb of "rat-ta-tat-tats!"

Chicago will probably never live down its gangster-era reputation. To make matters worse for me, after high school we moved to Cicero, once-home of Chicago's other favorite gangster son, Al Capone.

We were on "relief" in those early Depression years, along with a quarter of America's families. Once a month a government truck drove onto the block and needy families such as ours got potatoes, rice, oatmeal, raisins, and prunes. Lots and lots of prunes. Today, I can't look at a prune.

In the first few years of the Depression, the only work my father could find was selling ice cream bars. He pushed a little Good Humor ice-box-on-wheels out to the corner of 63rd and Halsted Street, near where we lived on the South Side at the time, and rang the little bicycle thumb bell for customers.

Even when I was only four years old in 1934, I felt sorry for him because, at the end of the day, my brother Johnny Boy who sold the same kind of ice cream at his Good Humor cart on an opposite corner wound up the day with more nickels and dimes than my father. I never could figure out why people felt sorrier for a boy of eight selling ice cream for a living than they did for a man doing the same work.

My brother got his little boy nickname because my father's name also was John and, instead of calling her first son Junior, Mom called him Johnny *Boy*.

The following summer, my father finally got a real job. Roosevelt's "New Deal" helped form The Works Progress Administration in 1935 to give jobs to the nation's eleven million unemployed. It was intended "to help men keep their heads up and their hands in," and included building and repairing roads and bridges.

Dad got a W.P.A. job helping rebuild Archer Avenue on the Southwest Side. We were living in the second floor apartment in the back of a building near Ashland Avenue and 38th Street.

The kitchen floor slanted so much, if I put a marble on one side of the room, it rolled down to the other. The soup always spilled out of one side of my bowl. My Uncle Stash who lived with us off-and-on, remedied the problem by folding a piece of cardboard under the low side of my bowl, to make it more level. You'll learn all about Uncle Stash in the next chapter.

When school let out that summer, Mary Jane and Johnny Boy and I took Dad his lunch, walking a couple of miles to where he was working. We sat on a cement curb he helped build the day before and visited with him. I liked playing with the wet clay there, molding it into cars and airplanes while we talked.

My mother found work, too. She got on ironing shirts in a Chinese hand laundry. It was hot that summer, and the laundry didn't have an electric fan much less air conditioning, so Mom arrived there early each morning, hoping to get an ironing board close to the door or a window. It couldn't have been much fun ironing shirts for eight hours with a hot iron when it was 90 degrees outside and probably 120 degrees in the laundry.

Later, she went to work for the Campbell Soup Company, breaking chickens apart or peeling potatoes. She got paid by the weight of the peeled potatoes minus the weight of their skins so, to make the skins come off easier, the women peeled them under cold water. The work gave Mom a bad case of arthritis she suffers from to this day.

On Fridays, Mary Jane and Johnny Boy and I walked several miles to where Mom worked and met her when she got her pay envelope. She took five dollars of it in cans of soup. They were dented "seconds," but inside the soup tasted just as good. We helped her carry home the heavy bagsful of cans, never spending money on streetcar fare.

My mother saved the little round plastic rings that were put on the feet of the chickens she cut up. They were in various colors and we kids had fun linking them together and making make-believe necklaces out of them.

I searched for flowers to give to Mom on those Friday visits to the factory where she worked. One day on the way there, I saw some yellow wildflowers in an empty lot. They looked beautiful to me so I picked a handful of them and offered them to Mom as if they were rare varieties of flowers. Years later, my sister told me what they were. They had been only dandelions. But my mother accepted them as if they had been orchids.

Also that year, 1935, we began playing a game Aunt Mary brought to the apartment when she visited. She came around more often than any other aunt or uncle and soon became our favorite. In no time, like the rest of the country we were all hooked on the game, Monopoly. It was a board game about buying real estate and becoming rich, dreamed up ironically enough by a jobless inventor. He made so much money on the game, he stopped looking for work.

Some of the most fun I had as a boy was when Aunt Mary played Monopoly with us children. She was not only hard of hearing but often a little slow on the uptake. If our token stopped on a space she owned and we owed her rent, we purposely waited longer than usual to see if she would notice it. She studied the board for the longest time but usually failed to see where our tokens landed, until just as we shook the dice to roll our turn. Then she came to as if exploding out of a cannon, crying out, "*My property*!" While collecting her rent, she giggled gleefully.

If people weren't playing Monopoly, they played bingo, at church parlors and on the screen in movie theaters, hoping to win a lamp or some dishes or a dollar or two.

Mary Jane was the reader in the family. After school and doing her homework, she curled up in the high-backed stuffed chair in the parlor and read *Little Women, Anne of Green Gables,* or some other book. Johnny Boy and I didn't read much unless we had to, for school.

In 1936, when I was six, a book came out that might have helped me at the time, but I didn't know about it until years later. Businessman Dale Carnegie's book, *How to Win Friends and Influence People* , took the country by storm. My problem was not so much how to win friends as how to hold on to them. It was because we moved so much.

The strongest memory I have of my boyhood is sitting on the tailgate of a truck, waving good-bye to my friends. We moved almost every year, from one apartment to another, from one neighborhood to another, sometimes halfway across Chicago, more often just a mile or block or two away.

I didn't have to ask why. I just knew from hearing Mom and Dad talk that we were moving so they could find a better apartment in a better neighborhood. They all looked the same to me.

Years later, my brother told me the real reason we moved almost every year. Our folks couldn't make the rent payments and the landlords always asked us to move. I realize now that even eight or ten dollars a month for rent was big money back in the mid-Thirties.

But I hated moving because I didn't want to leave my pals behind. I had hardly met them, then had to lose them.

I've forgotten who they were, and only remember the little boy whose father was a doctor. My friend was rich enough to have his own tricycle and sometimes he let me ride it. He seems to be a composite of all the pals
I waved good-bye to as we moved away.

Most of my friends were boys, but I still can visualize the first girl I fell in love with. Her name was Patsy and she had long brown hair and the prettiest face I'd ever seen. We were in first grade together at a South Side school, and when our class picture was being taken I planned to be looking at her.

I was one of the tallest boys in the class, so I was in the back row, and Patsy was sitting in the front row, so I could only look at the back of her head. But when the photographer snapped the shutter on his speed graphic camera, I was looking somewhere else. It seemed for some reason to me proof that Patsy and I would never get together, and we never did.

I must have been only about six when I suffered two of life's most bitter disillusionments. The first happened on Easter Sunday, 1936.

Neighborhood merchants and parents organized a big Easter Egg hunt in a local park after Mass that day. They hid hard-boiled colored eggs, chocolate bunnies, toys, and baskets full of goodies behind bushes and trees for us kids to find. I didn't find a single egg, so I began to cry. Mary Jane and Johnny Boy found candy and toys everywhere they looked, so afterward my mother took pity on me and gave me some of their findings. It was the only time I ever got anything for crying.

The second big disillusionment came that Christmas. We lived in an apartment with a fireplace even though it didn't work and the house got heated by two coal stoves, one in the kitchen and the other in the parlor. The previous Christmas Eve I cleaned the base of the chimney so Santa Claus wouldn't get the white fur on his red coat dirty when he climbed down it that night to leave us kids our presents. Mary Jane who was seven and Johnny Boy who was nine laughed their sides out when I began sweeping around the bottom of the chimney the next Christmas Eve.

Afterward I asked my mother for a cup of hot cocoa which I wanted to leave for Santa, just as I had the year before. That made my brother and sister laugh even more.

"You don't still believe in Santa Claus, do you?" Johnny Boy asked me, doubling up.

I looked to my sister for some help but found, to my dismay, she couldn't stop laughing.

I got the message. I didn't need a ton of bricks to fall on my head. According to the two know-it-alls I lived with, I had been laboring under a pair of delusions all my years. They decided it was time for me to grow up and face reality.

"Then," I said haltingly, the thought wounding me deeply, "if there's no Santa Claus, isn't there an Easter Bunny either?"

It's hard to forgive some people some things. I can still hear my brother and sister laughing and am not sure I forgive them yet, after half a century. I don't think I was quite ready, at age six, for that double-whammy of reality.

Chapter Five

I'm waiting for ships that never come in

Whenever I see one of the city's street people today, I think of my Uncle Stash.

His name was Stanley Kowalski, as in *A Streetcar Named Desire,* but he was tall and skinny and didn't look anything like Marlon Brando, especially with his shirt off. I even had an aunt named Stella, though she was married to another uncle named Steve and not to Uncle Stash.

To the Polish, the names Stanley and Steve not only are popular, they're interchangeable. The men my uncle worked with called him "Whitey," because of his hair, but to my brother and sister, my parents, and his other relatives, my father's black sheep uncle was always Uncle Stash.

He never married and was one of a small number of bachelor uncles and aunts who played a very special part in my life. Remembering them makes me think that maybe it's a good thing that more young people today are waiting longer to get married, and some decide not to get married at all. How are kids today going to learn anything about life, if they don't have colorful aunts and uncles who may be a little extra independent and want to live life their own way that often is not in a nine-to-five job?

Off and on in the years shortly before World War II, Uncle Stash lived with us in the flats we rented in various parts of the city.

He was one of a vanishing breed, a gandy dancer on the railroads, during the Depression years of the 1930s and early 1940s. Gandy dancers were members of railroad track crews. They got their nickname by laying track and ties and driving steel spikes with hammers made by the long defunct Gandy Manufacturing Company. Today the work is modernized with automatic spiking machines and gandy dancers are called trackmen. They're also probably not as colorful as Uncle Stash.

His job was to cook for the men who repaired the rails out West of Chicago in states such as Nebraska and the Dakotas and Colorado. They sounded very far-away and adventurous to a city-bound grammar school kid like me. Among other things, I learned some geography from Uncle Stash, because he told us stories about his travels around the country.

I remembered Uncle Stash best in the early 1940s. I was still in grammar school when the family lived on the North Side near Division Street and Ashland and Milwaukee Avenues. It was one of the largest and oldest-established Polish neighborhoods in Chicago.

Mom said Uncle Stash used to baby-sit for us kids over the years, when she and Dad were working. He liked things quiet around the house and, when we cried as babies, he had his own peculiar methods for quieting us.

One night my mother smelled liquor on our breaths. Stash said he gave us a short snort of bourbon, so we would go to sleep. When I was just a baby, Mom came home from work one night and caught Stash putting my head in the oven, with the gas on. That also was supposed to put me to sleep.

Uncle Stash never wrote or phoned to announce his arrival at our house. One day, he just appeared, like an apparition.

Our flat above a candy store on North Marshfield Avenue was entered from a street-level front door that led up a long flight of stairs to the second floor. There was a long hallway that divided the rooms and one day when we just about forgot we had an Uncle Stash, he materialized there. In those days, people seldom locked their doors, so he just came on up. But he never made a sound when he entered. He was quiet as a ghost and usually even looked like one, his face the color of an old unbleached towel.

His arrival was always the same. "Uncle Stash!" Mom cried. "You nearly scared me to death! Why don't you cough or walk heavier, so we know you're here? You're like a cat!"

Stash would hand my mother a bottle of wine as a present, then shake his right leg. As if shaking off bad luck, he'd say, "*Jeje* boat!"

It was Polish for "Here comes the ship!" and meant, "My ship's going to come in!"

Uncle Stash and most of our family was always waiting for their ship to come in; their fortune to be made or their bad luck to turn. Our ships never did come in. The bread we cast upon the waters always came back soggy.

That was just one expression Stash frequently used. Another was, "You can't tell a book by its cover" and, whenever anyone threatened him, he boasted, "I never took a back seat for nobody!" meaning he was always in the driver's seat.

Yet another of his favorite sayings was "It's a *pashkudny* case," meaning it's hopeless. When he had enough of someone, he told them, "Sit down before you get knocked down!"

Usually Uncle Stash showed up near the end of winter, and would be sick. After working all summer and early fall on a railroad crew somewhere out West, he got paid, but was broke again. Railroad workers, many of whom were heavy drinkers back in the prewar Depression days, didn't get paid in cash. Their pay was held in escrow until the season's end, when they would get it all in a fat envelope.

While they worked, they were given free housing and meals. But their pay was deferred until the end of the work season. Instead of a weekly paycheck, they got chits which they could exchange for harmless items such as toothpaste, soda, candy, and Bull Durham for making their own cigarettes, but no cash money because they would just spend it on whiskey or wine. Muscatel was mother's milk to Uncle Stash.

Many gandy dancers didn't go home after they got their season's pay. Some may not have had homes or loved ones to go to, while others didn't have the courage to face those who might be at home waiting for them.

Uncle Stash had brothers and sisters in Chicago so he came back to the city, but seldom saw them. At least not when he still had money in his pocket, and they didn't want to see him when he was broke.

When he had money, he went to South State Street and spent it in the bars, then slept his benders off in flop-houses. When his money was spent, or someone had jackrolled him, he sat between some buildings in an alley somewhere to nurse a hit on the head or a stomach sloshed with wine that made him sick.

He made sure you knew the class distinction between bums and hobos, and between the type of men who frequented South State Street and those who made West Madison Street their home. The Madison Street crowd were bums. They wouldn't work but panhandled for their drink money. A better class of men of misfortune hung out on South State Street. They were hobos, not bums, and they worked odd jobs to earn their drink money. Uncle Stash made sure you credited him with being a hobo from South State Street, not a bum from West Madison.

After returning from a season as a gandy dancer cook and losing his money one way or another, one day he would take a streetcar over to our house and just appear in the hallway like a phantom. Mom would get over her fright and give him a cup of hot black coffee, then send him to bed and start to nurse him back to health with chicken soup and kindness. His own family might turn him away when he was broke and ill, but Mom who was not blood kin, never would.

When he was well again, Uncle Stash then would become part of our household and family, for as long as he wanted to stay. He kept the house spotlessly clean by sweeping and dusting and never let a dirty dish remain in the sink after a meal. He also took over Mom's chore of cooking while she went to work each day. He cooked "mush" (oatmeal) for us kids in the morning, looked after us when we came home from school in the afternoon, and prepared the evening meal.

His way of looking after us after school was simple. He just locked us out and told us to play outside. We played in the street until supper time because we were miles from the nearest playgrounds at Wicker or Eckhart Parks.

Even when it was below zero out, Uncle Stash never let us in the house to warm up or even use the bathroom. If we somehow managed to get in and raided the cookie jar, he came after us, swinging a broom. So we played in the street, bounce-or-fly with a softball and bat if we could scrape them up, or slammed empty cans on the heels of our shoes and galloped around like racehorses on the brick streets. Or we wandered up the alleys looking for colored shards of glass to collect in old cigar boxes, or tried to find discarded Popsicle sticks that might have "Free" written on them, to take to a store and exchange for a free one.

While staying with us, Uncle Stash spent his days listening to baseball on the radio, as this was long before television. He listened to two games at once, keeping score for each. He followed the Cubs on the Philco console in the parlor and the Sox on the Zenith portable atop the ice box in the kitchen. Shuffling back and forth from one end of the flat to the other in my father's house slippers, he recorded hits, runs, and errors with pencil and notebook, always carrying a cup of steaming black coffee with him.

Between innings, he chopped up vegetables and braised stew meat for a supper dish he called "slumgullion." It was a stew made up of anything he could find in the ice box, and usually was hot and stuck to our ribs.

While he remained with us, Uncle Stash never drank and always watched his language. He kept his mind busy on baseball and his fingers occupied rolling his own cigarettes. And he read the newspaper thoroughly, with a pair of reading glasses that slid far down on his nose. He bought his glasses for twenty-five cents at the corner drug store.

Stash was usually gruff with us children, but we knew he loved us and his stern nature was just a cover-up for a soft heart towards us.

In his own way, he was helpful, such as when he propped up my soup bowl with cardboard so it didn't spill in the slanty kitchen.

Somehow, Stash was never quite flat broke. He always had a few nickels and dimes on him that he gave to us kids to buy treats with.

Sometimes he told us stories about his adventures. The one that stuck in my mind the most was about working one summer out in Colorado. He got his season's pay when the first cold winds began to blow and the work was done for that year, boarded a train, and came back to Chicago.

Another gandy dancer he worked with that summer rode the train home with him, a younger man he called Jim. It probably wasn't his real name because many gentlemen of the road worked under aliases, trying to closely guard themselves against any possible ties to their past.

Jim was on the thin side too, a good-looking blond young man in his early thirties, sunburned and healthy from working outdoors all summer. He had taken the job on the railroad because he was down on his luck and the pay was better than any job he could find in the city. Jim told Stash he had a wife and kids he was going home to, with his season's pay. But he was nervous about facing her and asked Stash if he'd have a drink with him first.

They went to State Street just South of the Loop and were sitting at a bar having a couple of farewell drinks when Jim suddenly remembered he had an envelope fat with cash money in his pants pocket. When he took it out and waved it, Stash got up and started to leave, cautioning his naive young friend not to show that he had money on him. Someone might take it away from him.

About two weeks later, Stash was still cruising around State Street with some money still left in his pockets when he saw someone coming toward him who looked vaguely familiar. But he couldn't place the man, who had a stubble of beard on his once handsome but now careworn face. The approaching man's clothes looked dirty and slept-in, and he limped from a game right leg.

Stash looked away as the man started to pass him. The stranger surprised him by calling out, "Stash! Don't you recognize me?"

Stash stopped, studied the face, then recognized it. "Jim! What happened to you?" he asked.

The disheveled young man took Stash aside and told him his story. After they had parted that night two weeks before, some men had followed Jim out of the bar and beat him, then took all his money.

"What are you going to do now?" Stash asked.

Jim lowered his head and nearly cried. "I'm broke, so I can't go home. I guess I'll try to live through the winter here somehow. Then, in the spring, I'll go back out West. I'll work on the railroad again. Maybe if I try it all over again, I'll have better luck."

Stash tried to talk Jim into going home to his wife. "She'll understand," he said. "She'll take you in."

Jim shook his head and started to walk away. "I couldn't go home. Not without any money, and the way I look. Good luck to you, Whitey. Maybe I'll see you out in Colorado next spring."

Stash never saw Jim again, although he worked with a lot of men just like him, year after year.

He told us stories like that and they were the kind we never forgot.

Some days, Stash went grocery shopping with my mother. After they got back home, he pulled things out of his pants and coat pockets. Things like a can of corn, a box of cookies, or a length of Polish sausage. Sometimes, even a bottle of wine, for her and my father.

"Stash, I didn't buy those things!" Mom told him.

"Don't worry about it, Pauline," he replied.

"Don't ever shoplift when I'm with you!" Mom admonished. "If I knew you were taking things, I'd have been a nervous wreck in the store!"

Stash stayed with us until, one day after a month or more, he would be gone. He never told my father or us kids he was leaving, but the night before he left, he would tell Mom. He asked her for whatever she could spare to get him started again, even if it was only a few quarters or a dollar or two. And he asked her for a warm coat. Maybe he would use the coat, maybe he would sell it, for a bottle of muscatel.

My mother rummaged through my father's and brother's clothes and outfitted Stash as best she could. Once after he left us, when I was in high school, I looked for a shirt I was hoping would become one of the hand-me-downs I usually got; something my father would hand down to my brother and, when I grew into it, it would pass down to me.

I had seen my Dad wear a light green soft silk shirt which one of his brothers had given him. Dad had only worn it a few times, then handed it down to my brother. I waited, wanting that shirt more than anything, until finally it would be worn enough and I would grow enough, so it would be passed down to me.

Before that could happen, Uncle Stash came to stay with us. When he left a few months later, I didn't see the green silk shirt anymore and asked Mom about it. "Oh," she said offhandedly, "I gave that to Uncle Stash before he left." To her, it had been almost a rag, only worth covering a poor hobo's bones. To me, that shirt was as beautiful as Jacob's Technicolor dream coat.

I was left with a bad case of wanting. Ever since then I've looked everywhere for a shirt like it, but never found it. It took years before I could forgive my Mom and Uncle Stash for my not getting that shirt. Finally, I did. Maybe. What not getting that shirt did was, it made me a shirtaholic. I began collecting shirts like Imelda Marcos collected shoes.

So Uncle Stash would leave again and we knew we wouldn't see him again until he had been gone for about a year and was broke again and sick.

This went on through my grammar school and into my high school years. Then one late fall when I was in my junior year and the war had started in the Pacific and Europe, he came back to our flat. This time he looked especially gray and ill.

"Stash, you look like you've got T.B.," my mother said.

He coughed hard. "Oh, I had that. I was at the County Hospital for a few days, but they let me go. I guess I still got it."

Tuberculosis had taken the lives of too many people Mom loved. Hating to turn him away, Mom said, "Stash, I'm sorry but I can't let you stay with us if you've got T.B. I can't take a chance on the children catching it."

Stash shook his right leg. "*Jeje* boat!" he said as a parting salutation. That was 1942 and the last we ever saw of Uncle Stash.

About five years later, one of his sisters was dying. "Before I go," she said, "I'd like to see Stash once more."

One of my aunts tried finding Stash and even hired a private detective to trace him. It wasn't an easy task. There were so many lost souls wandering across the country in those years, there was a popular radio program called "Mr. Keene, Tracer of Lost Persons" that we listened to every week. Now my Uncle Stash was one of those.

After a few days, the private investigator reported that he located a man answering Stash's description. He was in the morgue in Los Angeles. Aunt Josephine, my father's oldest sister, was about to fly out and look at the body when the detective called again.

An aside about Aunt Josephine. She was another of my favorites. All my aunts were really my favorites. Aunt Jo was always really nice to me and the other kids in the family, but had a temper she sometimes took out on her husband. Once, according to family lore, she got mad at him at a family poker party and threw a kitchen knife at him that found its way into his arm.

Another time, while my father and mother were driving us home from one of the weekend family poker parties and dropping Aunt Josephine off at her apartment, she joked as we were close to letting her out near a train tunnel. She said we'd better leave her off under a lamp light or the *Chicago Tribune* headline the next morning might read, "Glamour Girl Found Dead Under the Viaduct." I thought that was hilarious.

Back now to the private detective's phone call about missing Uncle Stash...

"Forget about L.A.," he said. "I think I found your uncle, in the Cook County morgue right here in Chicago."

Reluctantly, Aunt Jo went to the morgue and viewed the remains of the man believed to be our uncle. The man had the bad luck of falling out of bed in a flophouse on South State Street ("that great street") on a below-zero night. He'd hit his head on the hot radiator and hadn't been discovered for several days. He was about Stash's age and build, but because the face was so bloated and he had no identification on him, she couldn't be sure it was our family's Stanley Kowalski.

I'm sorry this part of Stash's story isn't prettier, but that was how he lived and apparently how he died. I say apparently because the family wasn't a hundred percent convinced that the man who got a good Polish funeral and who is buried in Resurrection Cemetery in Southwest suburban Justice is our Uncle Stash.

The body of the man who might have been him was claimed and he was given a burial befitting any other member of the family. But a lot of relatives were never quite sure, looking at the face of the man in the casket at the wake.

Was he our Stanley Kowalski? He could have been anybody of our uncle's build and age who had the misfortune of falling out of bed in a flophouse in Chicago that cold winter night.

Years later, my brother told me, "I was driving down Milwaukee Avenue in the old neighborhood last week and saw an old, skinny, gray-haired man standing on a street corner. His back was to me, but he looked just like Uncle Stash."

Aunts, uncles, and cousins have told of similar sightings over the years: "You know, many times I've seen men who looked just like Uncle Stash." "I wonder if we buried the right man?" "I wonder if Stash is still alive somewhere?"

Is he still roaming around Chicago? By now, surely not. If he were alive, he'd be in his nineties. But then, Aunt Jo just died and she was 94.

In our family, the mystery goes on. As my brother has said, "I just wonder. Did we bury our Uncle Stash or did we bury somebody like him?"

What did I learn from Uncle Stash? When we kids were writing or drawing, he was frugal and always told us to use both sides of a sheet of paper. And he taught my brother and me that no matter how coarse our lives were, never to swear or speak improperly around women.

By example more than instruction, Uncle Stash taught us to be careful how much whiskey or wine we drank. And not to boast you have money because somebody might try to take it away from you.

To this day, I kind of hero-worship Uncle Stash because he was, more than anyone I've ever known, his own man. He was the first truly independent person I ever met and did things *his* way. He may have disappointed many in the family, because he chose a lifestyle that didn't lead to him being a success, in any traditional meaning of the word. But to me he was a success. He lived a life of freedom and to my knowledge never hurt anyone.

Maybe the black-sheep free spirit of the family had an even greater influence on me than I realize, because I grew up to be fiercely independent. Uncle Stash may be the reason why I chose the free but uncertain life of a freelance writer.

One of the main things Stash taught my brother and sister and me was to live and let live. He cautioned us many times not to make judgments about others by saying, "You can't tell a book by its cover." That's what I think about most when I see some of the homeless, the men and women today who for one reason or another live on the streets.

Stanley Kowalski pretty much chose that way of life. He had been On the Road long before Jack Kerouac thought of trying that kind of lifestyle. But Stash would have been the first to tell him that lots of others didn't live without a home by choice.

Knowing Uncle Stash makes me think that these street people today may be my uncle or aunt, or yours, because, in one way or another, we're all related to each other. We're all part of the same family, whether we feed our own or someone else's, or bury them.

Chapter Six

Happy days are here again

Words can't describe the way the Stock Yards smelled on the South Side when Chicago was "hog butcher for the world." All I know is, when we moved there in 1936, my nose never smelled anything that bad in the six years I'd had it. I can still smell the Stock Yards, almost 80 years later.

We lived near Ashland Avenue and 38th Street, several miles away from the open pens where cows and pigs were kept and then slaughtered for the tables of that minority of Depression-era Americans who could afford to buy steaks, roasts, and hams. But you could smell the bulls and oinkers as much as if you were standing right in the stalls with them, especially when a South wind blew.

Those first few days after we moved there, we smelled nothing else. But as things have a way of happening, we soon began to get used to the smell and, eventually, hardly noticed it. When relatives or friends visited and asked for a clothespin for their nose, we asked what they were talking about.

Besides the smell, about the first thing I remember moving to that neighborhood was Mom getting me into a pair of Doctor Denton's, the one-piece flannel pajamas with the trap door in the rear. Before we went to bed on winter nights, she gave us a cup of hot Ovaltine.

The next thing I remember, our folks took us to Riverview, the big amusement park that packed them in on the North Side every summer with roller coaster rides, spook houses, and chalk kewpie dolls we won if we tossed a ball at some wooden milk bottles and our aim was good.

Mae West was one of the queens of the movie screen back then and had become famous for telling a gentleman suitor, "Come up and see me sometime." My mother coaxed me into doing my Mae West impersonation one Sunday we went to Riverview, for a couple of hundred people having lunch in the pavilion.

I was a chubby little platinum blond dumpling and, even back then, a ham. Getting up on the stage, I put a hand on my hip and started to slink across with a little shimmy while I recited the famous line and brought the house down, or the pavilion.

Back then, girls wore low-wasted dresses, long white stockings and patent leather shoes, and ribbons in their hair. Boys wore plaid wool knickers and high-top laced boots, and a Boy Scout camping knife usually went free with the boots. We wore flat-top caps just as grown-up men did. The caps are fashionable again today, another proof that what was old often is new again, if you wait long enough.

On hot, sweltering summer days someone got a wrench and opened up a fire hydrant. Then all of us boys and girls on the block stripped down to our underwear. We tried to get as close to the hard-gushing spray of water as we could without falling down. Backing into it, of course.

After a while, someone called the cops and they shut off the water. Then we splashed around in what was left in the gutters, or sailed little wooden sailboats toward the sewers, catching them just in time. Those without sailboats launched Popsicle sticks.

By then the ice man came by with his horse and wagon. While he was inside someone's house delivering a 25 or 50 pound block of ice, we raised the tarpaulin on the back of the wagon and climbed inside, chipping off some chunks with his ice pick. As he came back, we would be running up the street with a shard of ice to suck on and cool us off.

The ice men always had younger and healthier-looking horses than the rag men, whose horses looked to be just one step away from the glue factory. But we liked the rag men's horses best. They wore a frayed, old straw hat or a floppy felt one with slits in it so the horse's ears poked up through it.

There were good things to eat back then. The corner drug store sold penny candy and my favorites were chocolate "frying pans" on a stick, jawbreakers, tiny wax bottles with syrup inside, and licorice strips, especially red or brown rather than black. Our flat on the second floor in the back of a building was heated by a coal stove and, in winter, my brother and sister and I scorched our licorice strips on it. If we let a strip of licorice get hot and start to melt on top the stove, it began to bubble and scorch. Then we put it outside a window and let it freeze. You've never eaten heaven until you've eaten scorched, brittle licorice.

If we didn't have candy to eat, which was often, we made open-faced sugar sandwiches. That was some sugar sprinkled on top a slice of white bread. Johnny Boy had his own variation of that. He made a condiment sandwich, spreading mustard, horse radish, and catsup on a slice of bread. Mary and I never cared to try it.

If we had a cold, Mom made us some of her wonderful cough syrup. It was a mixture of hot water, lemon, honey, and rock candy. If she had some whiskey or wine in the house, she added a little of that. We kids used to fake having colds, just to get a cup of her elixir.

But the taste treat of those days was something very special that happened only once a month. On Thursday afternoons, the National Biscuit Company a few blocks away on Ashland Avenue sold cookie "seconds." These were slightly bruised or broken sugar wafers, vanilla and butter cookies, fig bars, chocolate marshmallow pinwheels, and half a dozen others of our favorites that in those days would never get packed into a box to be sold. They went instead into five-pound brown paper bags and sold for twenty-five cents the bagful.

Johnny Boy and Mary Jane and I scraped up a quarter by redeeming empty soda and milk bottles or running errands for merchants in the neighborhood and stood in line to buy the huge bag of cookies. Then we sat on a curb and my brother divided them up... one butter cookie for Sis, one for me, one for him; one chocolate marshmallow for her, one for me, one for him until the bottom of the bag was reached. If only one or two cookies were left, he broke them up so each of us got an even share.

We sat wolfing down the cookies until the last one was gone and we began to feel sick. When we went home, Mom guessed why we didn't have an appetite for supper. She always seemed to know when it was our time of month and understood.

Running errands was sometimes fun as well as being lucrative, for candy and soda or show money. Except when we ran errands for the doctor whose office was above the drug store on the corner. His assistant, Blanche Krushka, was a midget and we liked her but didn't care much for how she paid us for running her errands. Instead of pennies, she paid us off in parrot seeds. She had a caged parrot in the reception room that had a very salty vocabulary. When she wasn't looking, we poked at it, to tick it off. Then it sounded like a sailor on shore leave.

The druggist, a lady named Mrs. Kastetsky, was a thin, sharp-nosed widow of about fifty who had wavy gray hair. One day my brother told us a fantastic story about her. He said he had been at a rear window peeking into her bedroom one Friday after she closed up.

"I saw her take off her hair!" Johnny Boy told us. "She was bald as a bowling ball. Then she put on a red wig. A little later, she left, all dressed up and twirling her purse by its string, getting into a taxi."

It seemed, according to my brother, that Mrs. Kastetsky was a chameleon. By weekday she was staid and proper, wearing a matronly gray wig. But come Friday night, she became a scarlet-tressed woman in her red go-partying wig.

After that, it was impossible to look at Mrs. Kastetsky without imagining her totally bald.

Another lady in that neighborhood used to create another type of sensation. She was an old grandmother who came out of her house day or night and began cursing. She didn't seem to curse at anyone in particular, unless it was God, because she swore a blue streak as she raised an arm and shook it at the wind. We made a game of provoking her into cursing at us, until one day a neighbor told us why she was so strange. She had lost a son in the Great War and the loss had affected her reason. After learning that, we stopped taunting her, but she kept on cursing the wind.

The men on the block, except for one old man, were not as colorful. We called him Jadek, Polish for Grandfather, but he far from endeared himself to us. It was because we didn't live near a park so we played softball in the street. Whenever the ball got batted into his yard, which was several times a day, he came out of his house swinging a broom and yelled at us to go away. Grudgingly, he tossed our ball back. But before long, like a magnet, it got hit right back in his yard again.

Aunt Stella and Uncle Steve (not Stash) owned a house a few blocks away from the apartment we rented. She was a nice but very thin old lady and I only remember her one way... always on her knees, scrubbing the kitchen floor. While the floor was still wet, she laid newspapers over it. It was to keep her husband and son from dirtying the floor by walking on it with their shoes.

Aunt Stella didn't talk much, and had a standard reply for most any question or comment put to her. It was, "America, bullshit!" I never knew why she said that, except she had come from Poland and apparently liked the Old Country better.

Uncle Steve had an even smaller vocabulary. I never heard him say anything. Aunt Stella was the boss. She was smaller than him.

My uncle's hobby, kept on their screened back porch, intrigued me. It was a collection of snuff boxes. After he emptied a box's last pinch of snuff up his nose -- I supposed so he could breathe better or sniff something he liked to smell -- he stacked the box on top the others on the porch. The last I saw them, the boxes were stacked one on top of or beside the other until they reached from floor to ceiling around the whole porch, except for where the screening was.

I told you, some of my aunts and uncles did stupid things before they died.

Mom had four favorite expressions. One was, "Don't talk like a sausage!" Two others were horticultural sayings: "Sure as little green apples!" and "Money doesn't grow on trees!"

But the expression my mother used often that meant the most to me over the years was, "It'll all come out in the wash." She meant that no matter how bad things seemed, time would pass and any hurt would be healed; any misfortune wouldn't last forever but would eventually end. It was another way of saying: "Don't worry. Things always have a way of working out."

Holding fast to a philosophy that "Everything comes out in the wash" must have given Mom some comfort and hope after Dad gambled away his paychecks and left her wondering how to pay the rent and put food on the table. Somehow, we survived, month-to-month. It came largely from charging most purchases, from furniture to groceries.

The bills that were run up caused a lot of arguments between my mother and father over the years. It wasn't any fun for my brother and sister and I to hear them, so we left the house when we could. Johnny Boy ran away from home a lot, because of the arguments. He stayed away until after dark, then came back only because he was cold or hungry.

When our folks were getting along okay, they were sometimes lovebirds and we liked seeing them that way. Mom was dark-haired, slim, and to us, beautiful. Dad was six-foot four, solidly built, and handsome. They made a very good-looking couple walking us to church every Sunday. Especially when Mom wore a new spring hat she would make herself each year, and Dad wore a new straw boater. With prematurely graying hair and wearing a navy blue suit to church, everyone said my father looked distinguished, like a policeman or a detective.

Dad had a sweet term of endearment for Mom. He called her "Shoog." It was short for "Sugar."

It was many years later that I learned where that came from. Dad said one of his favorite actresses in the late 1930s and early 1940s was Glenda Farrell, a good-looking blonde. She became known for playing a wise-cracking hotshot newspaper reporter, Torchy Blane, in a movie series. Her boyfriend in those movies, Barton MacLane, a detective, called her "Sugar." Mom and Dad sometimes took us kids to the movies and we loved that.

Johnny Boy had a word for a girl who had a crush on him in grade school when we lived on the South Side. He called her "Scum of the Earth." Somehow, it never discouraged her from making eyes at him. Maybe it was because he was growing tall, dark-haired, and handsome.

As he grew into his teens, Johnny Boy became a dead-ringer for a younger version of one of our favorite new actors, Ronald Reagan. Little did we know then that the actor with the winning smile would become President of the United States and that some people would think he made a great president while others would think he should have stayed an actor.

We had two nicknames for my sister. Johnny Boy called her "Saxophone Sis" or "Booth," which was short for "phone booth." Mary Jane never played a saxophone or got hit by a phone booth or had any other special contact with one that I know of, so I never knew why he gave her either name.

Dad called Mary Jane "Sis," and she was his favorite. Sometimes she and I fought like cats and dogs, but despite our arguments, she also was my best friend when we were growing up. That was partly because we were alone together so much, when Mom and Dad were both working and my brother was with his friends or just away somewhere in the neighborhood.

Sis was terrified of cats. It was because when she was about five and we lived in a basement apartment on the North Side, she was sleeping in her bedroom off an alley with the window open on a warm summer day. Someone tossed a cat onto her bed and she woke up with it on her chest, spitting at her.

Maybe Johnny Boy did it. He did things like that. Often for no reason, he just went after me. Sometimes after school, when Mom and Dad were out working and we three kids were home alone listening to "Jack Armstrong" or "Terry and the Pirates" on the radio, he threw me face-up on the couch in the parlor, then stomped on my stomach with his feet. I was too little and young to get back at him, and always wondered, while I tried catching my breath, why did he do that?

I fought back as best I could, being almost four years younger, but usually my clashes with my brother were verbal and not physical. He yelled at me about something and I yelled back, "Oh yeah?" It wasn't much of an offense or defense but, after all, he was bigger.

As far back as I can remember, when our folks weren't around, our brother was in charge of my sister and me. The one thing we never minded was when he took us to the neighborhood Goodwill Center on Tuesday nights. It was part of the Goodwill Industries, a charitable organization in the city. It helped plenty of needy people during the Depression and still operates used clothing and furniture stores and helps feed and clothe the poor and homeless.

Tuesday was Movie Night at the Goodwill Center a few blocks away from where we lived. Neighborhood boys and girls got to see a feature movie that usually was a cowboy picture with Tom Mix or Buck Jones. They also showed an episode of a serial (we called them "chapter-plays") such as "Rin-Tin-Tin the Wonder Dog" or "Tailspin Tommy," and a Popeye or Betty Boop cartoon.

Not a boy or girl would think of leaving before the chapter play, which was always last on the program, so the local merchants who ran the show took advantage of their captive audience to slip in a commercial. Before each week's chapter play installment, while we wondered if the hero or heroine got untied from the railroad tracks as an express train approached full-throttle, a local doctor or druggist or preacher was invited to lecture to us boys and girls. Always on the same topic: the evils of alcohol.

Prohibition was over, but the Goodwill people were still against drinking. It was probably because many of the down-and-outers they tried to help had gotten that way from too much whiskey, wine, or beer. One way Goodwill fought against alcoholism was to ask local leaders of a community to lecture to us kids about the pitfalls of drink.

My brother, who seldom stayed where he was supposed to, ventured out of his seat in the darkened Goodwill hall one night just as our neighborhood dentist started giving his sermon on Demon Rum. Johnny Boy reported back to us in our seats just as the chapter play began, after the lecture,

"I saw the dentist behind the movie screen and he took a snort out of a gin bottle!"

We were never again able to keep a straight face during the Goodwill temperance lectures.

The movies at the Goodwill center were the biggest bargain in town. Admission was only two cents a head. Once my mother sent us there and Johnny Boy handed the ticket-taker a dime for three admissions. The man had to send out for change.

One afternoon while watching a movie at one of the neighborhood theaters I asked my brother, "Are the actors and their cars or horses and everything else on the screen really on the stage behind it?"

"Yeah, sure," he said, and of course I believed him.

Johnny Boy laughed for days over that, then scared me silly the next time we went to see a chapter play. I had been comfortable enough watching the villain harass the hero for eleven episodes of a thrill-a-minute serial. In the final installment, the bad guy tried escaping over a deep gorge, going hand-over-hand over a rope extending from one side to the other.

"Who *is* that bad man in the black suit?" I asked.

"Don't you know? That's Bela Lugosi!"

I knew who *he* was. He played Count Dracula! Just hearing his name and knowing the actor crossing the gorge was him was enough to make me curl up on my seat with my legs under me and close my eyes tightly. After waiting for eleven weeks, I couldn't muster the courage to watch the last five minutes of the chapter play.

My brother did things like that.

But despite that, the three of us were close. As we began growing up, we helped each other work a newspaper route or go for firewood.

We lived about two miles from some freight yards where railroad cars were uncoupled and left on sidings. It was south of Archer Avenue and west of Ashland Avenue which later became a large railroad produce market terminal, along the Chicago Sanitary and Ship Canal. Beneath the Archer Avenue bridge was "No Man's Land," a shantytown where drifters and bums lived as best they could and warmed themselves on cold nights over fires they built in old metal drums.

Johnny Boy had a paper route along Archer Avenue and I often went along and helped him. He especially needed help carrying the coaster wagon he took along to hold the papers in summer, or a sled in winter. It seemed like a thousand zig-zag wooden steps from the freight yard shantytown up to the top of the bridge, but together we always made it and never lost a paper.

It was no place for children to be, especially after dark, but in winter we needed firewood to start the fires in the coal stove at home and there wasn't any money to spare for such luxuries. So every week in winter, one day after school, Johnny Boy and Mary and I took our sled and went hunting for kindling down by the railroad freight yards a couple of miles from home.

When the temperature fell below zero, we bundled up so our mouth and nose had a scarf over them, though our toes felt frozen. Sometimes we trudged through snowdrifts to get to the train yards. When we finally got there, always after dark, Johnny Boy told us to hide behind some trees or boxcars along a siding and wait with the sled until he called us. Then he went ahead and scouted out the boxcars, looking inside them for loose wood.

The railroad people didn't want anyone hanging around the trains, so they always had guards on the look-out for kids or bums on the road looking for a way to hitch a free ride to another part of the country. We always had to be careful no "spotter" saw us.

When Johnny Boy found a freight car with enough wood to take a chance on taking, he waved to us. Mary and I ran across the tracks pulling the sled behind us, bringing it down under the boxcar he was standing in, hiding from a spotter. Fast as Johnny Boy could, he tossed the wood down to us and we stacked it on the sled. When there was a full load, we roped it down and pulled the sled over the tracks and out of the yard.

Besides watching out for spotters, we also had to keep an eye out for moving trains. Engines were always pulling into or out of the yards, coupling or uncoupling boxcars, and there were so many tracks, we were never quite sure which one had a train on it, heading our way. A locomotive's bright light would blind us, making it hard, if not impossible, to tell which track a train was on.

One night, my brother tossed down a pile of wood from a Phoebe Snow boxcar. My sister and I hurriedly stacked and tied it to the sled. Johnny Boy began pulling it across the tracks, and Mary and I followed. As we started heading out of the freight yards, the bright light of a fast-approaching train began blinding us.

"What track's it coming on?" Sis asked anxiously.

"Darned if I can tell!" Johnny Boy called back.

In the dark and the blinding light, the train could be on any one of the tracks we were crossing. All we could see was, it was bearing down on us, and fast.

Johnny Boy looked at the situation fast, then pulled the sled to the left side, which he thought was safe. Seconds before the whole night filled with the light of the oncoming engine, he pushed Sis and me to the left. The train rumbled by us on iron wheels, on the very next track we had just jumped from.

A freight yard spotter saw us then, aiming his flashlight at us. We ran fast as we could, Johnny Boy not forgetting what we came for and pulling the sled behind us.

On the way home, taking turns pulling the sled, we agreed we wouldn't tell Mom or Dad about our close call, and tried forgetting how frozen our toes felt.

Before we moved the next summer, when I turned eight, Mom realized she had never thrown a big birthday party for me. She and Aunt Mary got to thinking of a theme. It was 1938 and we had just seen Errol Flynn, my favorite actor, in "The Adventures of Robin Hood." They decided to throw me a Robin Hood birthday party.

First they took up the carpet and cleared all the furniture out of the dining room, moving table and chairs and china cabinet into the living room. Then, with very little money to spare on decorations, they set about transforming it into Sherwood Forest. They bought some green crepe paper and cut out trees and bushes which they thumb-tacked onto the walls. It was June and hot, so they opened all the windows.

The party was a huge success, even though my father was not there. He had taken that occasion to get in a poker game after work with some friends. It was a habit he had gotten into for some time, staying away on a lot of holidays and our birthdays. When he came home a day or two later, he was broke, having lost most or all of his pay on cards, and was sick from too much drink.

My neighborhood friends all came to the party and Mom and Aunt Mary made green paper Robin Hood hats for each of us to wear and served ice cream and cake. There were games too, such as bobbing for apples and pin-the-tail-on-the-donkey.

After the party, it was so hot that night and Mom and Aunt Mary were so tired, they left everything as it was. They would put the dining room carpet and furniture back the next day.

It was the best birthday party I'd ever had, and I slept well that hot summer night. So, apparently, did my father.

My mother found him the next morning, curled up asleep on the floor in the dining room. She gently shook him awake and, forgiving as always after one of his nights out when he blew in his pay, she asked,

"Why did you sleep on the floor? You know you could have come to bed."

Dad leaned on an elbow, stretched his legs out, and looked lovingly at her. "Shoog, I'm sorry. When I got home last night everyone was in bed and the house was so hot. Except for this room. There was a breeze and the moon was shining in through the windows... I thought I was in a forest. So I fell asleep under the cool shade trees."

How could Mom not love and forgive him, again?

Chapter Seven

That old black magic

Chicago is full of ghosts and haunted houses, and so is my family. My brother and sister and I learned about them, since they haunted some of the neighborhoods we lived in.

Adam, the whistling ghost, for example. He's not on the polling sheets at City Hall and doesn't send out for pizza, yet at least four people swear to his presence, making him one of Chicago's most visible ghosts-about-town.

A young family was moving into a house in Old Town, an older part of Chicago's North Side. The husband, named Ted, told my sister, brother, and me,

"Our little boy was coming up from the basement one day whistling a tune and it puzzled my wife and me. He'd never whistled that or any other full tune before. When we asked what he was whistling, he told us, 'My friend Adam, in the basement, taught it to me.'

"My wife and I went and looked, but there was no one in the basement. Yet, after that, we felt the ghost's presence down there."

Ted said that one night at a party in the house, a guest suddenly bolted out of the living room. When asked what was the matter, he said, "If that guy in the chair in the corner doesn't stop staring at me. I'm gonna punch him out!"

"The thing was," Ted said, "there wasn't anyone sitting in the chair. But when the guest was told the chair was empty, he described a young man sitting in it with blue eyes in his late teens, dressed in denim pants and sports shirt."

A neighbor at the party said, "That was Adam. A young man who was murdered in the house some years ago."

"Shortly after that," Ted told us, "some friends were over and we were in the living room. Suddenly we all saw a strange light in the room and had the feeling of a spirit's presence. Then our dog howled and ran to the back door, scared to death and wanting to get out of the house."

Adam stayed with the family in Old Town for about two years. During that time, things were missing from time to time and he played games by ringing the doorbell. The family learned to live with him, though the dog never did. Then one day they sensed that Adam had left, to go whistling somewhere else.

Another ghost in Old Town haunted a house on Sedgwick Street, a block from another flat we lived in. An old woman who said she saw the ghost told us kids,

"I was about to go down in the basement with my bulldog one day when suddenly someone laid a hand on my shoulder.

I heard a woman crying deeply, as if warning me not to go down there. Our dog is short-haired, but when his hair stood up and he wouldn't go downstairs, I figured I'd follow his good judgment and stay upstairs. That hand on my shoulder was enough for me!"

The woman said her daughter Jennie was alone in the house one day when she noticed an image in a full-length mirror in a closet door. It was the reflection of a girl about twelve years old with long blonde hair done up in braids. She was in a long, white, puffy-sleeved dress such as children wore back in the 1880s.

"The house is full of spooks," the woman told us. "Sometimes the piano or phonograph start playing all by themselves. You can pull the electric cord out of the wall, but the phonograph still plays. It even plays records we don't own!"

St. Michael's Church in Old Town, only a block from where we later lived, had one of the scariest ghosts.

Father "Curly" Miller, who performed exorcisms in the city, was leaving the church one night when he noticed an old woman behind him. He held the heavy wooden doors of the church open for her, and as she passed outside, he noticed she had no feet. The priest said the woman had hooves, like the devil when it appeared as a cloven-footed animal.

Another supposedly haunted church was St. Rita's on the Southwest Side. One year on the night of All Soul's Day, about a dozen parishioners were praying for indulgences for lost souls. Suddenly the organ began playing, by itself.

The worshippers looked behind them to see six hooded figures floating above the choir loft, three in white robes and three in black. When the ghosts began gliding down to the floor of the church, the faithful below ran for the exists, but found them to be locked. When they looked back, the figures were floating through the pews. Suddenly, the church doors flew open by themselves, and everyone ran out.

Ghosts have haunted both the Polish and Austrian sides of my family, from as far back as I can remember.

The first ghostly visitation involves Uncle Stash. It happened in 1927 when one of my father's younger sisters, Theresa, died while in her teens.

Back in those days, the deceased might not be waked at an undertaking parlor but at home. This might be done to save on funeral expenses or because a more private, family setting was desired.

Doubtlessly for economy's sake, Theresa's wake was held at Grandma's house on South Peoria Street. A wreath was hung outside the front door of the two-story red brick bungalow and her body was laid out in a casket that stood on a catafalque in the living room. Sliding "pocket" doors could be closed and locked between the living and dining rooms. According to tradition or superstition, all the mirrors in the house were covered, apparently because the deceased's reflection might be seen there.

Catholic wakes, whether at funeral parlors or homes, lasted three days and nights and most still do. This is in order to allow time for relatives and friends in distant parts of the country to travel to pay their last respects to the deceased and offer comfort to the bereaved.

Family, neighbors, and friends gathered the first night of Theresa's wake and among the relatives who came was Uncle Stash. My father and mother joined the rest of the mourners at the wake. As always at Polish wakes in the home, food and drinks were served in the kitchen or dining room.

At ten o'clock, everyone knelt and said the Rosary in front of the bier and then left the living room. Grandpa George closed the sliding doors and locked them. They would be reopened in the morning when visitation would start again for the second day of the wake.

Some of the relatives went back to their apartments or houses and would return the next day or evening, after work, while others stayed overnight at Grandma's. With many of Dad's brothers and sisters still unmarried and living at home, the house was full and every bed in it was filled. Uncle Stash found himself sleeping on the couch which had been moved out of the living room and into the dining room, just outside and to one side of the pocket doors.

Sometime during the night, Stash heard some noises that awakened him. Shuffling and moaning sounds were coming from the other side of the pocket doors. He got up off the couch and tried the handle, but the doors were locked. Still, he heard the strange noises coming from the living room where the body was in repose.

Stash woke up the whole house. Grandma and Grandpa and Dad and his brothers and sisters, my Mom and everyone got out of bed in their night clothes. They gathered in the dining room where Stash stood in front of the pocket doors.

"I heard noises in there!" Stash declared. "But there shouldn't be any, because only Theresa's in there and she's dead!"

Everyone thought Stash had taken in a little too much muscatel that night, but to humor him, my father got the key and unlocked the doors. After sliding them apart, he and Stash and everyone else could see... Theresa still slept peacefully and there was no one in the room with her.

Dad tried the windows and found that they were all locked, from the inside. There was no other door in the living room except the pocket door. No closet, no other entrance or exit.

"You must have had a bad dream," Dad told Stash and everyone agreed.

"I heard somebody walking around in there!" Stash insisted.

After the pocket doors were locked again, everyone else went back to their bedrooms and Stash stretched out again on the couch in the dining room. He didn't hear any further noises and slept through to the next morning.

That night, it happened again. After everyone had gathered in the living room and said the Rosary for the repose of Theresa's soul, they went to their beds and Stash to his couch. During the night, he heard the shuffling and moaning from inside the living room and woke up the rest of the house.

Again Dad checked and found the pocket doors were still locked, the windows were too, and no one was in the living room with the corpse.

"I swear I heard someone in there, moaning and walking around!" Stash persisted.

Again the pocket doors were locked and everyone went back to bed. Stash took up a vigil on the couch until, not hearing a sound from the other side, he finally fell asleep and slept until morning.

The third night, it happened again. This time, when everyone got up and gathered in the dining room and Dad unlocked the pocket doors, Stash rushed past him and entered the living room. Everyone could see there was no one there except the body.

Stash began swearing a blue streak at whoever or what-ever he had heard in the room for three nights. "Whoever's in here," he shouted, "*go away!*"

Afterward, he tried the windows himself but found they were still locked, from the inside. He paused a moment at one of the windows and looked out.

Uncle Stash saw a figure in a long black coat, standing in the light of a lamppost down by the corner. He couldn't tell if it was a man or a woman.

He called to the others to look but when they did, they didn't see anyone there.

Stash insisted it was a spirit that had entered the room all three nights and visited Theresa, then left to stand watch on the corner.

No one could talk him out of what he said he heard and saw, so after Dad locked the pocket doors again, everyone went back to bed. Stash didn't hear any more sounds from the living room and slept until morning. Later that day, everyone attended the funeral Mass and Theresa was buried.

Who or what had awakened Stash all three nights during her wake remained a mystery.

Another ghost or spirit is said to have visited the house of my Aunt Helen, one of my father's cousins. It was a hot summer day in 1937 and her mother was upstairs in her bedroom, very ill.

Aunt Helen was downstairs in the kitchen, preparing

lunch. While she was at the sink, washing vegetables for a salad, she heard the screen door behind her open, then slam closed.

She turned and looked behind her, but no one was there. Opening the door, she looked into the back yard but there was no one there, either. Puzzled, she went back to the sink.

While her back was turned to the door, she began hearing strange sounds. Someone's feet were shuffling behind her, crossing the kitchen floor.

She turned and looked, but saw no one. Yet the sound of shuffling feet went past her and out of the kitchen, into the dining room.

Aunt Helen left the sink and followed the shuffling sound through the dining room and as it started to go upstairs. She followed the sound up the stairs and heard the walker go up the hall, then enter her mother's room.
When she went to the open doorway and looked inside, she saw that her mother had died.

As she went to her mother's bedside, she turned at hearing another sound. Not of feet shuffling, but more like a large, heavy box or bale of newspapers being dragged across the floor. It was moving out of the bedroom and into the hall.

Aunt Helen was too frightened to follow as she heard the dragging sound go back down the stairs. She stood at the top of the stairs and heard the sound pass through the dining room and across the kitchen floor. Then the screen door in the kitchen opened again and slammed shut.

She ran down the stairs and into the kitchen, but saw no one there. Again she opened the screen door and looked out into the yard, but didn't see anyone there, either. She never knew who or what had come to visit her mother in the final moments of the old woman's life.

My brother, sister, and I heard these stories told when we were young. Dutifully, we retold them to the next generation of young people in the family and now they can pass them on to their children and grandchildren.

But the ghosts or spirits didn't leave our family after those two. There were others whose visitations will be told in the next chapters.

Chapter Eight

I'm always chasing rainbows

When I was eight, in 1938, we moved from the South Side to the North and lived in an apartment on Evergreen Avenue in an old Polish neighborhood near Division Street and Elston Avenue. It was just a few blocks west of Chicago's only island, an industrial area called Goose Island.

Goose Island has been called the ugliest place in Chicago. I suppose the main reason we moved near there was the rents must have been cheap. Then, too, Aunt Stella and Uncle Steve had moved near there. My mother had begun to count on borrowing a few dollars from her at the end of the month when Dad gambled his paychecks away and the rent was due.

The island was once an uninhabited flat marsh that arose where the Chicago River separated into two banks for an eight or ten block stretch on the city's near Northwest Side. Irish immigrants were the first to settle on Goose Island, in 1847. The geese they raised there gave the island its name.

In 1866, a year after the Civil War ended, the city's first bridge, a wooden one, was built over the island and it started to become a place for factories and railroad yards. Fires and fumes from a gas company plant that extracted gas from coal created an eerie bluish glow which hovered over the island. People began calling it "Little Hell."

Lumber, stone, and coal yards, and later huge grain elevators were established on the island and the Irish squatters moved farther north in the city.

For many years, Goose Island had been the haven for thieves, thugs, and petty criminals. At one time the police considered it the most troublesome place in Chicago. Today Goose Island is renovated and considered a trendy place to live. Goose Island beer is a best-seller.

When we moved to Evergreen Avenue within a few blocks of it, Goose Island had become just another rundown industrial district. Today the John F. Kennedy expressway cuts through the old neighborhood.

There was a big empty lot next to our apartment and Johnny Boy and Mary Jane and I met our friends there after school and built bonfires. We got three potatoes from home, poked a stick through them, and roasted them over the fire at night, swapping ghost stories.

Those hot potatoes roasted in their skins are still about the best things I ever remember eating. Even when they fell off the stick and landed in the burning wood and we had to fish them out, burned black. Maybe they tasted so good because we roasted them ourselves and ate them with our pals around a bonfire with no "big people" around. We were on our own, in our own world.

A candy vendor pulled his horse drawn popcorn wagon onto the street on summer days and blew its steam whistle. We kids heard it wherever we were playing ball or alley-picking for bottle caps or colored glass for our collections. We spent a penny or two on treats from the wagon, if we had the money. We bought spun cotton candy or a taffy apple or a delicious thing that was two layers of thin waffle like a Communion wafer, only it had honey in between. Other favorites were a regular waffle covered with powdered sugar and sponge candy that melted in our mouth.

A weekly visitor to the neighborhood was the rag man. He brought his horse-drawn open wagon onto our street and called out something that sounded to me like "Rags-a-lie-eh!" It wasn't until years later that I learned what rag men called out was "Rags and old iron!" They collected rags and iron and took it somewhere to sell.

One day, the rag man invited me to climb up onto the seat next to him and ride with him around the block. I eagerly climbed aboard and had a great adventure riding with him. He took me for a ride around the block and it was the most exciting thing that had ever happened to me up to then. I'd never been that far from home without my folks or brother or sister before! Then the rag man returned me to the street I lived on, safe and sound. Today, he'd be arrested for suspicion of kidnapping a child to molest him.

Usually on Saturday mornings, another horse-drawn wagon pulled up on our block. It was the fruit and vegetable man selling fresh produce right from the South Water Street Market where trainloads and truckloads of potatoes, onions, lettuce, cabbage, apples and oranges were sold. Mothers and grandmothers on our block came out of their apartments and picked over the produce. It was like having a movable Farmer's Market right in front of our own house.

We bought some of our fruit and vegetables from the produce wagon, but when money was extra-short, Mom sent the three of us over to Goose Island. We wandered among the railroad boxcars in which produce had been shipped, looking for heads of lettuce or cabbage or other vegetables that might have been left behind. And we went to the warehouses where the produce was cleaned and packed. Women working there came to the windows and tossed us down some cabbage heads. We took them home and Mom made a good cabbage soup out of what we'd gotten for free.

Two other vendors came to our block regularly. One was the umbrella man who repaired broken umbrellas while customers waited. The other was the knife sharpener who had a hurdy-gurdy music box on wheels and a trained monkey to do tricks such as take its little hat off if we tipped it with a penny.

When we weren't scouting on Goose Island, we played out front of the house. If we had a bat and ball, we played baseball in the street, or "bounce or fly" (three catches and the batter's out). If we had some chalk we marked up the street or sidewalk and played hop scotch or sky blue.

If we didn't have anything to play with we played "Cops and Robbers" or "Cowboys and Indians," variations on the old "hide and seek" game.

Almost nobody had a bicycle. That was for rich kids. But one day Dad and Mom bought a new bike, for the three of us to share. Johnny Boy got to ride it first. Naturally, since he was the oldest. The first afternoon he had it, he rode it to the corner drugstore and left it outside when he went in to buy an ice cream cone. When he came out only a few minutes later, the bike was gone. Someone had stolen it. That was that. Dad said he couldn't afford to get us another.

Nobody had garage sales back then, where you could buy a used bicycle or anything. They didn't have a car much less a garage to keep one in. Besides, nobody ever sold anything secondhand. They used everything until it fell apart.

We did without bikes all the years we grew up. Our transportation around the neighborhood was by shank's mare or roller skates. Not the $80 models the kids today skate on with wheels on a blade like ice skates. Our skates had metal wheels and only cost a couple of dollars. They were strapped on our shoes and had clamps that could be tightened with a skate key. We were always losing our skate keys.

When the wheels of the skates were all worn down to practically nothing, they were called "hot boxes." They weren't good to skate on anymore, but weren't thrown out. Almost nothing was ever thrown out. There was always another use for everything.

"Hot boxes" were recycled as wheels for our push carts. My brother was good at making them. He got an empty orange crate from the grocery store and found some strips of wood in the alley. The strips would be sawed to about a foot long and an inch or two wide and he nailed them to the top of the crate, for handles. Next, he nailed the crate to a length of two-by-four about two-to-three-feet long.

Finally, two "hot box" roller skates were nailed onto the bottom of the two-by-four. If we were steady and fast enough, we could get pretty good mileage by putting our right foot on the two-by-four and the left on the street and pushing ourselves forward. When two or three push carts were on the street, we held races.

We decorated the front of the crate with bottle caps to spell our names or initials. During World War II, we shaped the bottle caps into "V" for "Victory."

Years later, my brother Johnny built a push cart with a crate and 2x4s and roller skates, to show his four young kids how he played when he was a boy. They wouldn't touch the thing. "It isn't store-bought!" they cried in unison. So much for showing his kids what it was like in "the good old days."

Our old push carts are the ancient forerunners of today's metal skate boards with metal handle bars, some of them even motorized. I wonder if they're as much fun to ride as our old orange crate push carts?

I was always too young to play my brother's favorite game, "Slaughteroo." A bunch of boys got together and picked out one of the group to be "It," then everyone else jumped on top of him. They wrestled him to the ground, punching and kicking, and tearing his clothes off. Many's the time my brother came home with his pants and sweater torn, his nose bloody, and his face red from punches. Boy!, I thought. Did he have a good time!

In winter, we had snowball wars or went sled-riding on the street. The most fun was just after a heavy snowfall, when the wooden front stairs were covered with snow. They were high stairs to a second floor apartment and we turned them into a sled slide.

The three of us shared one sled. My sister and I took turns sitting on it at the top of the stairs while our big brother stood behind us and gave us a good push-off. Then we soared down the snow-covered stairs, across the sidewalk, and out into the street, always on the lookout for passing cars.

Johnny Boy loved to give a little twist to our shoulders, just as he pushed us off. Instead of sailing down the stairs, we tumbled down sideways, head over sled over feet.

Once, I tried belly flopping on the sled when my brother gave me a good push-off. I went like lightning down the stairs and out into the street when I saw a truck coming.

I had a quick choice to make. Try to zoom under the truck, between its wheels, or try to turn away and not get hit. I tried that and just missed piling up against the side of the truck. It was something else we all agreed not to tell Mom about.

When the three of us kids got into fights with each other, Mom tried to keep order or punished us with a slap on the rear end. If we were really bad, she applied a strap there, and she had a pretty good swing with it. If we were worse than really bad, she told Dad when he came home from work. He gave us a good talking-to and maybe for good measure used his belt on our behinds.

My brother and I were always to blame for whatever fights we got in, never our sister. Especially to Dad. He always told us, even when Mary had caused it all, "She's the only little sister you have." Yeah, we thought. Thank heaven!

When Mom and Dad were working or not around, and Johnny Boy was in charge of us, he usually ignored us and went off and played with his pals. But sometimes he played with us and, at rare times, actually would be helpful.

One day my brother instructed me in how to walk correctly. "Don't walk like a duck, with your feet going sideways," he said, showing me. "Walk like this, with your toes pointing straight ahead. It looks better."

Several years later, when Mary and I were teenagers, she took over instructing me in things like that. She told me I had "B.O." (body odor). I guess I was kind of casual about washing under my arms, and she told me about it.

When we lived by Goose Island, our father was working in garages as an auto mechanic. He loved working on cars and was real good at it.

We didn't see our mother much during the week and on some weekends because she had returned to Illinois Bell and was a telephone operator again, but her hours and days on duty were irregular. If she couldn't be home for dinner, she made the meal for us in the morning before she left for work, or the night before, and Mary would heat it up for us.

Uncle Stash stayed with us for a few months on another of his unexpected and unannounced visits, and he did the cooking chores until he would vanish again. For a while, Aunt Mary came to live with us, and another time, my father's brother Leo lived with us. They were both out of work and needed a place to live while they looked for new jobs.

We didn't have to come home from school for lunch because there was a lunch program there. For about a nickel, we got a pint of milk and a sandwich and apple or, every few days, a hot meal. Our favorite was a hot dog and a plate of mashed potatoes with a little well in the middle into which was scooped some creamed corn. We mushed it all together and still like our potatoes and corn that way.

We went to public school, but always got off an hour early on Friday afternoons to attend Catechism lessons at St. Stanislaus Catholic Church, a few blocks west. In the church basement, a young priest taught us about the saints and we memorized prayers such as the Our Father and Hail Mary. We also learned the "Thou Shalt Not's."

I thought some of them were easier to live up to than others, especially "Thou shalt not kill," (that was easy; I knew I was tough, but not a killer); "Thou shalt not covet thy neighbor's wife" (that would be easy because I wasn't thinking of getting married); and "Thou shalt not commit adultery." I didn't even know what that meant, and the priest never said.

When it came time to make our First Holy Communion and Confirmation, the three of us made them all together. Johnny Boy simply had to wait until Mary could make hers, and they both had to wait until I could make mine. It was purely for economic reasons. Only one party needed to be held, instead of one for each of us.

My brother was mad at me when I made my First Communion because I got to wear long pants. Girls always wore white dresses for the occasion, and boys wore white pants, but when Johnny Boy made his First Communion, he had to wear "little boy" knee-length white knickers. Times changed in just a few years. The short pants fashion ended, thank heaven, and I got to wear long white pants. It must have been another reason my big brother took it out on me when he had the chance.

Dad still had the habit of not showing up for most parties, holidays, and family occasions like First Communion and Confirmation. He stayed away again for another few days playing poker and drinking with his pals. I kept wondering, if he liked being with them more than with us.

Sometimes he brought one of his pals home and we kids woke up in the morning and saw some stranger sleeping on the couch with all his clothes on. Usually, the man would never even be introduced to us. He just got up and left.

One of these men Dad called "Red" because of his hair. Red liked me so much, when I was seven or eight, he took me out and bought me a new suit and all kinds of clothes. Then he never came back.

If girls had liked me as much as some of Dad's poker-playing pals did, I'd have been as popular as Errol Flynn. But to tell the truth, I wasn't much interested in girls when I was eight, and even for a few years after that. Maybe it was because I was in love with someone up on the movie screen. I had fallen hard for Deanna Durbin, an angel-faced dark-haired girl who sang in her pictures and had a sweet if sometimes sassy way about her. I not only liked her looks and voice, but her spunk.

Shirley Temple was even more popular with moviegoers then, but I guess even then I liked older girls. Shirley was about my age, while Deanna was almost a teenager.

Now that I've brought up the subject of girls, and the logical progression from that is sex, I might as well report that my sex drive wasn't much until high school. It was probably because I had been brought up Catholic and had been told repeatedly by priests and nuns at Catechism lessons that it was a mortal sin to do almost anything to a girl beyond shake her hand or carry her books at school.

If we boys racked up enough mortal sins in our life, we'd not pass Go or collect $200 but go straight to hell. I figured no girl was worth that. Until at least I was in high school.

In place of or too young for real life sex, we went to the movies. At the nearly twelve movie theaters within waking distance of wherever our new apartment was, we saw the silver screen version which was romantic love, between Errol Flynn and Olivia de Havilland, Greer Garson and Walter Pidgeon, or Tyrone Power and Gene Tierney. They never took off their clothes and rarely even kissed, but you knew they were in love and, because babies usually followed, you knew they knew how to "do it."

The best times we spent with Mom and Dad were the week-ends when they weren't working. We spent them at my grandparents' house at 5207 South Peoria Street on the city's South Side. It was a regular family reunion.

After work on Fridays, all Dad's brothers and sisters who were married by then and lived around the city with families of their own got in their cars or rode the street cars, as we did, to gather at Grandma's and Grandpa's. Those who still lived at home joined us. It would be the start of another weekend poker game that lasted from Friday night all the way to Sunday night.

It was never necessary for anyone to make a telephone call to Grandma's and Grandpa's (the number was Boulevard 8-9882) to ask if there was going to be a poker game any weekend. There just always was. Besides, making a telephone call was not easy back then. We didn't have a telephone wherever we lived until late in World War II, when I was a teenager.

Mom would give me a couple of nickels every Saturday morning, to go to the corner drug store and sit in one of the phone booths there and make some calls. Most of them were to creditors. I would call the Gas Company to say we would be late paying our bill this month, but not to shut off the gas to our kitchen stove or oil stove in the dining room. I often made the same call to Commonwealth Edison, and to the L Fish Furniture Company that we would be late on the monthly time payment for our living room and dining room furniture and our beds.

The telephone at Grandma's and Grandpa's was in a hallway by their bathroom. My father's sister, Josephine, her young son, Tom, who was one of my favorite cousins, and four of Dad's brothers lived in the house with them. If any of them wanted to make a phone call or received one, the phone was on the wall in the hallway and it was hooked into what was then called semi-private phone service.

Private phone service gave you a phone and a monthly bill in the mail. With semi-phone service, there was a coin slot in a locked box where you put in a nickel to make a call. Once a month, a phone company employee came to the house, opened the coin box, and got the nickels.

No one ever even dreamed the day of cell phones was in our future.

Mom and Dad and my aunts and uncles took turns sitting in at the poker game on the dining room table. When some of the aunts weren't in the game, they prepared dinner, then served it to the aunts and uncles playing cards. After the card players ate, while they kept playing, they turned over their seats at the card table to the ones who hadn't eaten yet and made dinners for them. We children ate with any shift we wanted.

At night, the poker players took turns sleeping. On Sunday morning, they rotated going to Mass. The game never stopped. Usually it was "penny ante," but with all the wild cards Aunt Jo liked to call, such as "one-eyed jacks," the pot could mount up, especially when they played for nickels and dimes.

When the pots would be really big, about fifty cents, tensions and tempers began to surface. We kids heard the grown-ups shouting at each other, accusing one or the other of cheating or bluffing. Sometimes they got into roaring matches and even fistfights.

Aunt Jo took her poker seriously. One night she threw a bread knife at her husband and hit him in the arm. She had taken offense when he won a pot by bluffing. There had been thirty cents at stake.

My cousins and brother and sister and I got in fewer fights those weekends than the grown-ups. We went to a movie or played outside during the day. At night, we sat around the house and listened to the radio or Johnny Boy told us stories. He liked to scare us with ghost stories such as "Room for One More." It was about the Grim Reaper, driving a black hearse drawn by two black horses, calling out that there was "Room for one more" inside. My cousins Joe, Kay, Joanne, Carl, and Tom especially liked it when I told them that one, in a bedroom with the lights out and in a scary voice.

I kept my cousins busy writing for a weekly family newspaper I started. We put a new edition together with family gossip each week on those card-playing weekends at Grandma's.

I was the editor, layout artist, and also wrote news items and features, but put my cousins to work writing news of their sides of the family.

The newspaper was printed on lined spiral notebook pages and contained news about who had colds or the flu, who went on a trip somewhere in or out of the city.

On Sunday afternoons those weekends at Grandma's, I sat in the parlor with Grandpa and listened to some classical music he liked to hear on the radio. His favorite program was Phil Spitalny and His All-Girl Orchestra. They played light classical pieces and each selection featured a different girl soloist, such as Evelyn and Her Magic Violin.

Grandpa George and I developed a special relationship while we listened to the music. It must have been the start of my love for classical music, although I also always liked it when on Saturday night at home Mom and Dad and we children would listen to the National Barn Dance on radio, with a bowl of popcorn.

That June we gathered in front of the radio to hear the sporting event of 1938. We eagerly awaited the round-by-round report of Joe Louis' fight with Max Schmeling. It was exciting but over almost before it began. The Brown Bomber defeated Schmeling in the first round to retain his championship.

Today, I doubt I've watched any televised boxing bout or other sporting event with the interest and concentration we all gave to listening to the Joe Louis fights on radio. Why is that? Because radio made us use our imagination more?

Johnny Boy and Mary Jane and I listened to the radio serials after school every day and followed the further adventures of "Little Orphan Annie" and "Dick Tracy."

A few years later, when I was in high school and a couple of years before television, radio was the next best entertainment if we weren't going to the movies. Many times, it was even better. Mystery stories dramatized on the radio seemed even more spooky than the spookiest movie. When I listened to historical dramas on radio, such as "A Tale of Two Cities," I felt as if I was really in London or Paris, going up the stairs to the guillotine to get my head chopped off.

Also on those family poker game weekends, Grandpa gave us kids a haircut. He sat the boys down one-by-one on a chair in the kitchen while the card game was in full swing in the dining room, and put a cereal bowl on our head. Then he used scissors and his hair clippers and we got our ears "lowered." Grandpa never left any of our sideburns on. Today it's fashionable not to have sideburns. Back then it was a sign you hadn't gone to a real barber.

If we had a loose tooth, Grandpa tied a string around it and attached the other end to a doorknob. Then he opened the door and slammed it shut with such force, out came the tooth. Presto! No dentist bill!

If one of us fell down while playing and got a bump on the head, Grandma pressed a cold knife against the bump and it started to go down.

We kids were all pretty tired and yawning by the time eight or nine o'clock rolled around on Sunday night. We were glad when we heard an aunt say, "Let's make this the last hand," and the non-stop weekend poker game would finally end.

No matter how much they argued and fought since Friday night and the card game began, after the game, everyone stayed for about another hour. My mother and aunts cleaned up the dishes while Dad and his brothers gathered in the kitchen for some last few beers. Beer bottles in hand, they put their arms around each other's shoulders and did some barbershop harmonizing.

"Daisy, Daisy, give me your answer true. I'm half crazy, all for the love of you..."

"The bells are ringing, for me and my gal. The birds are singing, for me and my gal..."

"Let me call you sweetheart, I'm in love with you. Let me hear you whisper, that you love me too..."

"'Heart of My Heart,' I love that melody. 'Heart of My Heart,' brings back a memory. When we were kids on the corner of the street... We were rough and ready guys, But, Oh! how we could harmonize..."

And Dad's favorite,

"I'm always chasing rainbows, Watching clouds drifting by. My schemes are just like all my dreams, Ending in the sky..."

Dad could really relate to that.

After the harmonizing, everyone headed for home. We still didn't have a car, so went as we came, by streetcar. It was a long ride, back to the North Side. We transferred at street corners two or three times to zig-zag our way home. Sometimes on hot summer nights, sometimes in the rain or snow or freezing cold. We huddled in a doorway somewhere while Dad kept a lookout to see if our streetcar was coming. If we missed one, it might be half an hour or more before another came along.

The streetcars in those days ran on iron rails, with trolley lines above them attached to electric lines. There was an engine on both sides so the trolley didn't have to turn around at the end of the line. The seats were made of hard straw and could be flipped from one side to the other. When the trolley went as far as it could go in one direction, the seats were turned the other way for the ride back.

On the long streetcar rides, we kids busied ourselves with crayons and coloring books or looked out the window and counted candy stores or funeral parlors. When we were just babies and made those trips to Grandma's house, Mom used to take over one double seat and change our diapers on the way.

We would be on the streetcars several hours before we got home. It was always nine or ten o'clock or later when we started, so the trolleys weren't crowded and there were plenty of empty seats. We kids often curled up on a seat of our own and fell asleep.

Mom woke us when we were back in our own neighborhood on the North Side and approaching our stop. By then it might be midnight Sunday or even one o'clock on Monday, a school day. After our nap, we were still tired, but also hungry. Dad often took us all to a White City for chili and hot tamales.

Then we went home to bed. The next Friday, we did it all over again.

Chapter Nine

O Christmas tree, O Christmas tree,
How lovely are your branches

Big, fat snowflakes began to fall and stick to the barren branches of the Tree of Heaven growing outside our front window on Evergreen Avenue. Down below on the sidewalk I saw people hurrying by, carrying as many packages as their arms could hold, not seeming to mind the wet snow or the cold wind that sent shivers up my spine just being close to the frosty windowpane.

It was Christmas Eve, 1938, and there was no Yule tree nor any other sign of the season in the second floor apartment near the railroad yards. Dad wasn't home with his pay envelope. Unless he came soon, it didn't look as if there was going to be any Christmas for us.

Mom sat at the kitchen table with a cup of hot coffee while Johnny Boy and Mary Jane stood listening to carols coming from the radio on top of the ice box.

I kept my vigil at the window, pressing the palm of my hand against the cold glass every so often, to rub a place in the frost to look out. I wouldn't give up hope that Dad would come home before the clock struck midnight. He would have presents and a tree and good things for Mom to fix for us to eat. We would have a regular Christmas yet.

Of course, I was the dreamer. I was the one who had cleaned out the fireplace for Santa Claus the Christmases before, so he wouldn't get his red suit dirty with coal soot when he came down our chimney. And I was the one who had left a cup of hot cocoa for him besides.

Down deep, even I began to doubt that Dad would come home by midnight that Christmas Eve. He had stayed away for so many birthdays and holidays. Even when he came home, he wouldn't have any money left. He'd have lost it all in card games. Or if he won, he was always a soft touch for the pals he played with. If they lost and he won, they asked him for the loan of five or ten dollars and he gave it to them until he had little or nothing left himself to take home.

When he finally would come home, days later, he would be ill. But Mom could see that, and how ashamed and sorry he was, so she wouldn't scold him. She took him in and made a hot bath for him. She gave him some hot soup and sent him to bed until he was well again.

He wasn't only ill from drinking. Even at my age, I could see that. Something else was making him sick and made him stay away, but I didn't know what.

We kids would hear them talking in their bedroom. Mom would tell Dad that it didn't matter how much he brought home, so long as it was something and that he did come home.

That Christmas Eve, Mom finally got up from her chair at the kitchen table. She went to the closet by the front door.

"I'm going out for a while," she told us. "Don't wait up. I'll be back by midnight, if I can. And keep the fire going in the stove, but don't put too much coal in."

We were down to our last few bucketsful of coal for the potbelly stove in the kitchen, which had to spread its heat over the five-room apartment. It wasn't that big a flat, but even so our folks' bedroom off the parlor was always nearly as cold as it was outside. When the temperature fell below zero outside, the frost built up so thick on the windows in that front bedroom we couldn't see out.

My brother and sister and I didn't know where our mother was going, but we could guess. She was going to pay a call on Aunt Stella or someone, to borrow a little money.

"Want me to go with you?" Johnny Boy asked.

"No, it's all right," Mom replied, wrapping her thin cloth coat about her. Then she put on a *babushka*, a cloth worn on the head in place of a hat. She was slim and very pretty and none of us wanted her to go out. We felt alone enough.

"I'll be back soon," she said. "Keep the light on under the hot water tank. If your father comes home, make him a nice hot bath."

Mom left and we could hear her walking down the long flight of stairs to the front door. Looking out the front window, we watched as she walked up the street in what was turning into a heavy snowfall.

What she did and where she went that night I learned later.

She hadn't wanted Aunt Stella to know Dad was away, so she wouldn't ask her for any money. Instead she walked about a dozen blocks to a lady friend's apartment, someone she worked with at the telephone company, and borrowed ten dollars. It was a small fortune in those days.

A few small stores were still open around Division Street and Ashland Avenue. Mom walked there and bought some toys for us, and a duck which she would roast with the trimmings for Christmas Day. She had only about a dollar left to buy a Christmas tree, and set out looking for one.

But three strikes were against her. One, it was almost midnight, and few lots where trees were sold were still open. Two, it had been a bad season that year for Christmas trees and even little ones cost more than a dollar. Three, the neighborhood she was walking through was predominantly Jewish. There was little demand for Christmas trees.

Mom carried her packages and trudged through the snow from corner to corner looking for fir trees, but no one was selling any. The few lots which had sold them were closed up and the tree-sellers had gone home to celebrate their own Christmas Eve.

At less than fifteen minutes to midnight, Mom gave up on ever finding a tree. Chilled to the bone, and heartsick that we would not have a tree that Christmas, she turned around and started back for the apartment.

On the way home, she passed a Jewish delicatessen. She thought she might kill two birds: warm herself a minute, and ask about a Christmas tree. As she entered the shop, a little bell tinkled over the door.

Inside, she was reminded of her home in Landeck. The aroma of spicy sausages in the delicatessen was so much like that in the basement barn of the house in her birthplace.

The proprietor, a little old man in a bushy white mustache and white apron, leaned over the meat counter and asked,

"What are you doing out so late on Christmas Eve? You look frozen!"

"I'm looking for a Christmas tree," she told him. "I've looked everywhere, but all the lots are closed."

"I'm sorry lady," the proprietor said kindly, "but we have no Christmas trees." Then he added, almost apologetically, "It's a Jewish neighborhood, you know."

"Yes, I know," Mom said with a little smile. "Well, thank you just the same. I'd better go now. Merry Christmas."

"Merry Christmas to you, lady," the man called after her.

Mom shifted her packages in her arms and started to leave when a voice called to her from back in the shop. She turned to see the proprietor's wife, peeking her head out from behind some curtains leading to the living quarters in back.

"Excuse me, lady, but I couldn't help overhear," the small woman said. "A Christmas tree we don't have, but I'll show you... Come back a second and look."

Mom walked to the back room and looked at what the woman pointed to in a corner of their living quarters. A tall broad-leafed plant stood in a wooden pot.

"A Christmas tree it's not," said the woman. "But you're welcome to it for the holiday."

Mom gladly accepted the loan of the plant and let the proprietor help her adjust her load so she could carry it with her packages.

With some of the dollar she had left, Mom bought a small bottle of Mogen David wine and wished them Merry Christmas. As she went back out into the cold, a swirl of snow blew into the shop and she heard the little bell tinkle again over the door.

We children were asleep by the time Mom got back. It wasn't until Christmas morning that we saw all that Santa Claus had brought. There was a small pile of toys and games for us. Mom was in the kitchen basting a duck whose delicious aroma was already carrying through the apartment. In the living room stood the strangest Christmas tree we had ever seen, and the most wonderful.

Mom didn't tell us it was an India rubber plant. To us it was some strange and exotic kind of Christmas tree from some Eastern land where Jesus was born.

It was trimmed with tinsel and all our favorite ornaments from other Christmases. A string of colored lights was strung, criss-crossing the tree several times.

We were so excited, we hardly realized it when our father suddenly appeared in the apartment. He looked cold and tired and despondent. We knew he'd come home broke again.

Mom went to him and hugged him and we kids gathered around and hugged them both. It was going to be Christmas after all.

Mom opened the oven and we all looked in to see the duck roasting to a golden brown when it happened...

Dad backed up, somehow lost his balance, and sat down abruptly on the waist-high flat top of the potbelly stove!

The base was red and the top steamed as the seat of Dad's pants met it. He sat there only a split second. His face went red and he shouted something we didn't understand. He swore something in Polish as he leaped up reaching for the ceiling. Then he dashed for the kitchen door.

We all followed onto the back porch and saw Dad run down the long flight of wooden stairs against the back of the building. When he reached the back yard, he sat down in the cold, wet snow and began moving his rear end this way and that. The expression on his face told us he had found soothing relief.

Mom watched from the bottom of the stairs as Johnny Boy and Mary and I followed Dad out into the back yard, dropped to our rear ends, and began rolling in the snow with him.

It turned out to be one of the best Christmases, simply because we were all together.

Chapter Ten

Smile the while you kiss me sad adieu,
When the clouds roll by I'll come to you.
So wait and pray each night for me,
Till we meet again.

The following year, 1939, we moved again. This time it was only a few blocks away, west of Goose Island and into the heart of one of Chicago's oldest Polish neighborhoods, around Division Street and Ashland and Milwaukee Avenues. We moved into an apartment on Bosworth Avenue, just one block east of Ashland.

Around the corner was the Polish National Alliance headquarters and the official newspaper of the Polish community, the *Polish Daily Zgoda.* Dad spoke a little Polish only to his mother and father, but never at home, and Mom and we kids never learned it. Except for a few swear words. "Rotten eggs" and "dog's blood" sound a lot worse in Polish and we adopted them into our cussing vocabulary.

We walked down some cement stairs to get to the flat on Bosworth. They led down below the street-level to a long narrow gangway between our three-story brick building and another identical to it next door. We followed the gangway all the way to the end of the building where there was a little cement courtyard. Then there was a two-story building behind that and we lived up on the second floor of that building. How Mom and Dad ever found it in the first place was a wonder.

A few doors away, right next to an alley, was a little tavern where derelicts went to buy wine. One day an old woman walked up the stairs to the door of the tavern. She went in wearing a ratty coat and hat and came out a little later carrying a bottle in a paper bag, but she no longer had her hat or coat. She sold or pawned them for a bottle of wine which she sat down and drank in the alley, her back propped up against one of the buildings. The wine was probably as much nourishment as she'd get all day.

Compared to her, we didn't have it so bad. Our stomachs were never empty and we always found a way to get show money. At night, we listened to the radio, except when Commonwealth Edison shut off our electric service because our bill hadn't been paid.

When the lights went out, my brother and sister and I sat at the kitchen table to do our homework by candlelight, just like Abraham Lincoln had done before the invention of electric light. After doing our homework on dark winter nights, without the radio to help us pass the time, there was nothing else to do but go to bed early.

The year was not an easy one for most Americans, our family included. In 1939, eight million people were out of work. Dad was lucky to have gotten a job as an automobile mechanic at a garage he took the street car to get to because we had no car. Millions of men were still on W.P.A. (Works Progress Administration) jobs, building roads, repairing bridges, or just cleaning public areas, but Congress had to reduce their wages and set an 18-month limit on their jobs.

John Steinbeck's *The Grapes of Wrath* was published, telling the story of the Joad family of Oklahoma that was typical of thousands that lost their farms in the Depression and dust storms that followed the severe drought of the mid-1930s. They packed everything they could onto an old truck and headed for California in hopes of finding work there in the fields. All they found was hardship and disappointment, as migrant laborers.

Twenty years later, after I graduated from college and was a reporter for *The Chicago Tribune,* a younger friend from a wealthy suburban Detroit family who knew nothing firsthand about the Great Depression sat with me and watched a rerun of the movie of that book on television. Afterward, I asked what he thought of the tragedy of the Joads and the quarter of a million "Okies" like them. Disgusted, he replied with no compassion, "Why didn't they just go out and get jobs?"

I tried explaining that for most people there weren't any jobs to be had, but my young friend just couldn't seem to understand that. Maybe that's why today the words "Recession" or "Depression" don't seem to have the same meaning for those who didn't live through the 1930s.

Adolph Hitler's army took over Poland in 1939 and Britain and France declared war on Germany. I saw headlines about it in the newspapers, but being only nine years old, war in Europe seemed very far away and unreal.

Besides, I was busy with school and play. Or I was finding ways to earn pennies to buy bubble gum so I could add to my collection of baseball player cards. Another collection I was working on was bubble gum cards of Cowboys and Indians. Colored pictures showed scenes from famous battles such as Custer's Last Stand, with lots of blood all over the battlefield and arrows sticking out of the cavalrymen. Today's equivalent of that are cards showing Ninja Turtles, Batman, Dick Tracy, or whatever the latest block-buster movie is about.

That was the year I was double-promoted at school. The first day of school after summer vacation, classes were being assigned, but some of the rooms were so full, teachers promoted some of the boys and girls half a grade. I was tall, so the teacher in 4A promoted me to 4B. But when I reported to that class it also was too full. The teacher in 4B also picked me because I was tall, and promoted me to 5A. So I skipped a whole year in one day. I thought it was great, except I was never taught fractions, percentages, or decimals. I still have trouble with them. But who needs to know math today? We have pocket calculators for that!

Most of my memories of Bosworth Street are of going to the movies. There were about twelve movie theaters within walking distance of our house. Walking distance meant a couple of miles.

Going to see two new movies right from downtown still cost only a dime at the big neighborhood movie palaces such as the Crown or Biltmore. Lots of times, the older movies were just as exciting or as much fun and we could see three of them at the Royal for only a nickel.

That's where I saw my first real movie hero, stalwart blond Buster Crabbe as "Flash Gordon" in the serial. I couldn't wait each week for Saturday afternoon to come so Johnny Boy would take Mary Jane and me to see the next episode of Flash and his girlfriend Dale Arden trying to escape Ming the Merciless. Years later, even the high-tech rocket ship battles in "Star Wars" didn't excite me as much as when I had been watching Flash Gordon circle his tiny platinum space ship and land it on the sinister, dusty planet Mongo.

After Buster Crabbe, my favorites were Errol Flynn, the king of adventure movies, and a husky, cheerful he-man named George O'Brien who played a cowboy, logger, oil driller, or truck driver. He looked like and reminded me of Dad.

One night we went to see "The Gorilla," a scary comedy with the Ritz Brothers. I couldn't get to sleep afterward, thinking about the gorilla in the movie. As I lie in bed, I could see into the hall closet. Something big and dark was in there. I was afraid it was a gorilla. It kept me awake half the night. The next morning I saw it was only a coat hanging there.

Dad finally bought a car. It was used and bought on time payments, but we finally had wheels. It was great to drive out to Grandma's and Grandpa's in style instead of on a streetcar.

On some hot Sundays in summer, we drove to a lake in Indiana and went swimming. Mom made a picnic and after we ate, Dad stretched out on a blanket and slept until it was time to go home.

That summer, Dad bought a used old Nash and tried teaching Aunt Mary how to drive. Mom never wanted to learn. She said she never even could learn to ride a bicycle much less drive a car, her sense of balance was so poor. She seemed to think driving a car had something to do with balancing it.

I went along as Dad drove Aunt Mary to a cemetery early on a Sunday morning, when few cars would be there. When we got there, just to be on the safe side, he told me to get out of the car and watch from a distance.

I stood on a grassy slope amid some tombstones for people I didn't know, and watched as Aunt Mary got behind the wheel of the car and Dad sat beside her. Soon as she ground the gears I knew I was in for a good time.

She lurched the Nash forward like it was a bucking bronco, then stopped it dead. Dad's head nearly hit the windshield.

After a few more tries, Aunt Mary somehow got the car moving fairly steady and began driving it around some hills and curves in the cemetery. I lost sight of the car for a few minutes, then heard it before I saw it.

Somehow, Aunt Mary lost control of the car and it began speeding around a curve. It sounded like an airplane engine, the motor was so loud and running so fast. Then I saw it, heading right for me about sixty miles an hour.

"Put on the brakes!" I shouted, knowing full well Dad must have been telling my aunt to do just that.

Instead of slowing down or stopping, Aunt Mary drove the car faster. I figured she was so nervous, she got the brake pedal mixed up with the gas pedal.

I took no chances, as the car headed straight for me, and ran to one side. Aunt Mary turned the wheel and ran over a granite slab. Fortunately for the man under it, he was already dead.

Aunt Mary gave up on learning to drive after that experience. But years later, after burying her third husband and having no one else to drive her to church and the grocery store, she took lessons from a regular driving instructor. Then she became an even greater menace to the road.

We only had the car a few months. After falling behind in the payments, a skip-tracer from a credit agency came out and repossessed it. We kids were back to roller skates, push carts, and streetcars.

Aunt Mary had an apartment on Lincoln Avenue near the Biograph Theater. When we went there to visit, she and the folks played poker while we kids went to see a double feature.

Johnny Boy and Mary Jane and I got a good laugh out of one of the movies which reminded us of Aunt Mary's driving adventure in the cemetery. It was one of "The Falcon" series with Tom Conway as a private detective and he was in a cemetery at night, looking for a particular tombstone. When he pointed his flashlight at one slab, the epitaph said, "He raced for the railroad crossing, but the engine won." We kids laughed our sides out over that for about five minutes, until everyone else in the theater hollered at us to be quiet.

Once a year, Aunt Mary cleaned out her big old steamer trunk and let us children watch. There were lots of tiny drawers and hidden compartments in it and she took out her favorite things and showed them to us. Before closing up the trunk, she gave us some little thing. Once she gave me a tiny prayer book only about an inch square. It had about a dozen pages in it, a different prayer on each page. I still have it.

She also read books to us, especially chapters from *The Emerald City of Oz.* Her voice was soft and mesmerizing, like an encyclopedia salesman. While she read in soothing tones, I practically fell asleep.

Aunt Mary also told us funny stories about her friends. One, a tall, thin woman named Frieda Bodecker had trouble waking up for work in the morning, so she put her alarm clock in a dented pot beside her bed. When the alarm went off, it clanged and banged inside the pot, making enough noise to wake her and everyone else on the block.

At work one day, Frieda's boss got overly friendly. He came up from behind and hugged her so hard, he dislocated one of her ribs. It put her in traction in a hospital for a week.

Buck Genda, Dad's boyhood friend from Anderson, who also had moved to Chicago, married a nice woman named Edna. That Thanksgiving we were invited to a turkey dinner at their apartment not far from ours. I don't remember eating more than I did that day, before or since.

After the big meal, Dad leaned back in his chair and said, "I wonder what the poor people are doing tonight?"

He said that ironically after a good meal or something else good happened. It was ironic because he knew that if we weren't poor, we were about as close to it as anyone could get. Yet he felt rich because we were eating a good meal, we were healthy and, besides, we were all together.

I repeated that question of Dad's many times over the years, especially at Thanksgiving or Christmas dinners, and always wondered if he had made it up or heard it somewhere.

Just recently, in my seventy-ninth year, I happened to watch a video tape of an old movie, "Sunnyside Up," released in 1929. It was the first talking picture of the popular silent movie romantic team of Janet Gaynor and Charles Farrell. Gaynor played a poor girl, and in one scene was seated at a small table in her shabby apartment, having dinner with two friends. The dinner was meager but the friends were glad for it, when she looked up from her sparse plate and asked, "I wonder what the poor people are doing tonight?"

So that's where Dad had gotten the expression, from a movie at the start of the Great Depression. I remember many things my mother said to us, but that question at holiday dinners is the only thing I recall that my father ever said. In a way, it is enough.

Buck and Edna became like aunt and uncle to us kids and we saw a lot of them over the years. I liked their apartment because they had a shower in the bathtub. We didn't. We only had a tub. Every Saturday, Johnny Boy and I went up Division Street and took a shower at the YMCA. A small bar of soap cost a penny and so did rental of a towel. The water was free.

When Dad came home after having stayed away a day or two and didn't feel well from drinking, he went to another place near there, the Russian Baths. A long steam bath sweated out his aches and miseries.

Later that year, Dad had to stop working as a garage mechanic because he caught lumbago, a severe pain in the lower back. The garage he worked at wasn't heated very well in winter. His back became very sore from lying on cold cement floors, working under cars in cold weather.

He went to work in a factory after that, but one day some steel beams being transported overhead by a crane tipped and fell. One of the beams came down and hit one of his legs. He went to the hospital and was there for about a week until his leg was okay for him to walk on again. When we went with Mom to visit him we found wheelchairs no one was using and rode around the floor in them.

When he was better, Dad went to work for the Chicago Surface Lines as a bus driver. He worked a lot of night shifts and weekends, so we didn't see him as much then.

Sometimes Dad bought little things to give us. He treated each of us kids to a Milky Way or Three Musketeers chocolate candy bar or some little toy such as a pinwheel. We had fun blowing at the colored strips of plastic and watching them spin around. Once he gave us a gyroscope, a round metal toy that defied gravity by spinning in circles on the rim of just about anything, even a water glass.

One Valentine's Day, he gave Mom a big red heart-shaped box of chocolates and, for us kids, three smaller ones.

I knew Dad gave us the candy because he loved us, but it may also have been to ease his conscience, because he was still gambling and drinking and staying away a lot. Our parents quarreled more then and we children hated to hear them go at it. My brother must have hated it the most, because he began running away from home. He skipped school some days and went to the movies, not coming back until after dark, when he was tired and hungry.

About then, Dad stayed away for most of a week. When we asked Mom about it, she said he wasn't coming home. She said she couldn't take it any more. Dad's gambling and drinking had made him too unreliable. She couldn't count on him bringing home his pay any more. There were nothing but bills to pay and not enough money to pay them with since she could only depend upon her own earnings as a telephone operator. And there were just too many arguments.

My mother decided there was only one thing left to do.

Chapter Eleven

We strolled the lane, together;
You're gone from me; but in my memory,
We always will be together.

One night in the early spring of 1939, Mom told Mary Jane and Johnny Boy and me her decision. She was going to divorce our father. She still loved him, but could no longer take the strain of his drinking and gambling and the uncertain income that resulted.

Mary was nine and I was eight, and we missed Dad very much, after he and Mom divorced. We couldn't tell if our brother did, because he stayed away from home so much after school. By then he was thirteen, so Johnny insisted we drop the "Boy."

Lots of times, we thought he was in school, but he played hooky. He came home late and wouldn't say where he'd gone, but Sis and I figured he went downtown to a movie.

Mom didn't talk about Dad after they divorced. She didn't have to. We knew why she had wanted it. We just hoped that, somehow, they would get back together again.

We kept living in the apartment on Bosworth Avenue while Dad moved into the YMCA up Division Street near Damen Avenue. Some evenings, especially when Sis and I went to the Biltmore near there, we stood on the street across from the Y. Looking up at the windows, we wondered which room was Dad's.

After only a few months, Mom sat the three of us down on the couch, saying she had something to tell us. We hoped she was going to say that she and Dad were going to get back together again. But that wasn't it.

"I've met a nice man and we're going to get married," she told us.

It hit us like the roof fell in. If she got married again, that would be the end of it. She and Dad would never get reunited.

What could we do? We asked about the man she wanted to marry.

"His name is Otto," Mom said. "He's older and not very good-looking, but a nice man."

Our stepfather-to-be's name was hard for us to take. How could our mother give up our father for a man named Otto?

"And he's reliable," Mom said. "He doesn't smoke or drink, never gambles, and has a steady job as a mailman."

Best of all, it seemed to her, he owned a house, in a very nice neighborhood on the Northwest Side. She said it was a better house than any apartment we'd ever lived in.

We knew why she wanted to remarry. It wasn't because she loved Otto. He would be a steady provider and had a house. We would all have a roof over our heads.

They got married and we moved into Otto's brick bungalow on Melvina Avenue near Belmont and Austin Avenues. Ironically, our street was only a few blocks east of Narragansett Avenue where our real father was driving busses for the city.

Sis and I would rather have lived back in the old apartment on Bosworth with Mom and Dad, but Mom was right about one thing. Otto's house was the best we'd ever lived in, by far. We kids each had our own bedrooms and there was a refrigerator in the kitchen, not an ice box.

Otto's sister, who never married and had shared the house with him, didn't move out. At least not right away. Not until the sparks began to fly between her and Mom.

I forget our stepfather's sister's name but it might have been Cruella. We remembered what our Uncle Stash had told us kids, that "You can't tell a book by its cover," meaning not to judge someone just by their name or appearance. But she reminded us of the Wicked Witch of the West in "The Wizard of Oz." She was tall and skinny and always looked at us like she was sucking on a lemon.

We kids could tell she didn't like Mom because she was sure Mom didn't love her brother. But Otto knew that. Mom had told him, she still loved our father. She just couldn't go on living with Dad because the money he brought home was so low or undependable.

Otto accepted the arrangement. He loved Mom and hoped she and we kids would eventually come to love him. But we knew that could never be. So did his sister, who made it as hard on Mom as she could.

Otto's sister never tangled with Johnny or me, but made life miserable not only for Mom but for Mary Jane. She overloaded Sis with household chores and with a fetish about cleanliness, especially regarding her baby grand piano and large collection of knickknacks. Little glass and porcelain figures were on display all over the living and dining rooms on top tables and book cases, and inside glass-door cabinets. She made Sis dust them and polish the piano until Mary felt like her slave.

I didn't have any chores to do, but kept busy just trying to get away from Otto's three dogs. They were wire-haired terriers, two females and a male, and I couldn't tell them apart, but one of them kept jumping on me and trying to get familiar with me. I didn't like the dog that much and kept trying to hide from it.

One day all three of Otto's dogs got into a fight in the back yard and no one else was home. I was afraid they'd turn on me, so I turned the garden hose on them and soaked them until they stopped fighting.

I think Otto's dogs made me afraid of dogs, but thank heaven I got over that years later when I got my first dog, and became a dog lover.

Otto had a rock garden and pond and a little waterfall in the back yard, but kept it and the lawn so perfect, we children seldom were allowed there.

One cold, rainy April day, Mary Jane told me her shoes were so full of holes, she couldn't wear them to school another day. But the arrangement Mom had with Otto apparently didn't extend to him being generous enough to buy us children any new clothes. Sis would have to wait until Mom's next payday to get a new pair of shoes.

When Otto's sister learned of this, she offered a solution that may have been well-meant but didn't turn out to be any favor for Mary Jane. She loaned Sis a pair of her high-heel shoes.

Sis had no choice but to put them on and wear them to school. She could hardly walk in the shoes, the heels were so high, and they were obviously for an adult, not a little girl of ten. Sis could hear boys and other girls at school laughing at her and felt embarrassed, knowing she stood out like a girl dressed up for Halloween six months early.

The truth was, all three of us felt out of place, not only in the school but in the neighborhood. Sis had only two dresses, one of which she wore while the other would be in the laundry. Johnny and I didn't have much better wardrobes. We felt like poor relations because the other boys and girls on the block and at school dressed a lot better than we did.

After a few months, tensions between Mom and Otto's sister grew to the point where Mom asked him to choose between her and his sister. He chose Mom, and his sister moved out of the house.

Even with Otto's sister gone, Johnny and Sis and I weren't very happy. The neighborhood was the best we'd ever lived in, but we still felt out of place. Rich people didn't live there, but they made more money and lived better than anyone we'd ever lived around.

We didn't make any friends, around the house or at school. The kids seemed different. We sensed an upper-class snobbishness from the boys and girls both at school and on the block.

They also weren't as much fun as those we had gone alley-picking with or rode push carts with. These boys and girls had the best roller skates and bikes, but they didn't seem to have as good a time as Johnny and his pals when they played "Slaughteroo."

As we had before, living in poorer neighborhoods, we escaped to the movie theaters to forget our cares.

A Northwest Side premiere of "Gone With the Wind" played at the Will Rogers theater not far from our house, and we saw it there. The theater was like an Egyptian palace and we sat in plush seats in air-conditioned luxury, but somehow the beautiful theater wasn't as much fun to be in as the old Royal. There we usually sat in a broken seat with someone's gum on it, with only a fan moving the warm air around. But the Royal felt more like home to us.

Mom and Dad had agreed that he could see us a few times a month. Dad picked us up some Sundays and took Johnny and Mary Jane and me to lunch, then to the zoo or a ballgame. We had good times together, until it was time for him to take us back to Otto's house. Then it was hard to say good-bye. Especially when we saw the sadness in Dad's eyes. It made us think he missed us even more than we missed him. But we missed him an awful lot.

I have to give credit to Otto. Despite the fact none of us even liked him he tried to make us like him. He was just awfully bad at it.

The worst happened that Christmas. We never had been in a house decorated so much with a big Christmas tree and wreaths and holly, and a fire was burning in the fireplace. It might have been a nice Christmas, except for what happened when Otto handed out our presents.

The big Shirley Temple doll he gave Mary Jane was okay. Sis was eleven and still liked dolls. She hugged it to her and I thought, "You traitor! How could you like what you got from this man who will never be a substitute for our father?"

But I knew how she felt. She missed Dad probably more than I did, because she was his favorite. She just felt lonely and hugging the doll helped a little.

Next, Otto handed me my present. It was a box of something, I could tell by the feel of the cardboard under the gift wrapping. I knew from the size of it, like a shoebox, that it wasn't what I really wanted. But I had wanted that for more Christmases than I could remember and figured I'd never get it, even though each Christmas I dropped as many hints as our pilots later dropped bombs over Berlin.

What I wanted most was a toy typewriter. The kind where you pressed a metal circle with the letters of the alphabet on it. The circle would come down, ink a rubber letter, and print it on paper.

Opening the box, I forgot about wanting the typewriter. I never dreamed I'd get what was inside the box! It was a pair of shiny black hockey skates. I could hardly believe they were mine.

Otto let out a moan. "I'm so sorry, Wally," he apologized. "I must have put the wrong name on the tag. You're a little young for the ice skates. They're for your brother."

My heart sank. I had to hand the skates over to Johnny, and Otto gave me my real present. I hardly cared to open it. When I did, I found a set of Lincoln Logs inside. If Dad had given me a set of wooden building logs, I'd have loved them. But coming from Otto, after just losing the skates I'd loved to have had, I hated them. I've hated Lincoln Logs ever since.

The following week, Johnny and Sis and I rang in the new year at the Will Rogers. We saw "Here Comes Mr. Jordan," a really funny comedy about a boxer who had died before he was supposed to, and after the feature came a bunch of cartoons.

A few minutes before midnight, everyone began to sing, looking at some music on the screen and following a ball that bounced over each word in a song. It reminded us of Dad because the songs were all the old ones he and our uncles used to harmonize to.

"Happy New Year!" everyone shouted to each other in the theater when the hands on the clock on the screen were both straight up and 1941 arrived, on time.

Maybe the new year would be better. Maybe Mom and Dad would somehow get back together again. We could only hope.

The winter seemed longer than usual. I figured it was because the kids around Otto's house didn't get into snowball wars or ride their sleds down anyone's front stairs. They wouldn't have had much fun doing that, because all the houses were one-story bungalows and there were only four or five steps up to the front doors. To have any fun at all, you had to belly flop down at least two flights of stairs, as we had in the older neighborhoods we had lived in.

Our mother wasn't having any fun, either. She admitted to us that before she could go to bed with Otto each night, she had to take a shot or two of bourbon, to give her courage.

When spring came, Mom had something to tell us. It was just after school let out one day and Otto was at work.

"Your father has been writing me," she said. "And I've called him a few times. We don't know if we're going to get back together, but we've decided we all might go on a picnic this Sunday in Lincoln Park. Would you children like that?"

Would we like that? We could hardly wait for Sunday. When it finally came, Mom told Otto we were all going to visit her sister for the day. He may not have believed that, but didn't stop us.

We took a streetcar down to the lakefront and Dad met us at the restaurant by the Lincoln Park lagoon. Sis and Johnny and I hugged him and, after a while, we all walked up a grassy hill to a spot under some shade trees. Mom spread out a checkered picnic tablecloth and Dad arranged a blanket on the grass.

"You children go down and watch the row boats for a while," Mom told us. "Your father and I have some things to talk about."

Johnny and Sis and I went back down the hill and watched people renting row boats and taking them out onto the lagoon. Every so often, we looked back up at the hill. Mom and Dad were sitting close to each other on the blanket, holding hands. She looked extra-pretty in a summer dress with flowers printed all over it, and he looked real nice in a suit and tie.

After about half an hour, Mom called to us and we ran back up the hill.

"Your father and I have decided to go back together," Mom said.

It was the miracle we kept wishing for.

Chapter Twelve

Somewhere over the rainbow...
And the dreams that you dare to dream
really do come true.

Mom had always worked like a one-woman team of Polish housekeepers, cleaning an apartment before we left it. After packing everything we owned, she cleaned the flat we were moving from, sweeping and dusting, then scrubbing the floor in every room. After arriving in the new apartment, she cleaned that one just as thoroughly.

When we moved from Otto's house to an apartment on Marshfield Avenue back in the old neighborhood, she did something different.

My mother was not a vindictive woman. She didn't believe in getting back at people who did her wrong. In the case of Otto's sister, she made an exception.

Maybe she was just taking her frustrations out on the unfriendly woman, but the morning of the day we left Otto's house, Mom told Mary Jane and Johnny and me that we should help her make a mess of the place. We weren't to do any structural damage, but some ketchup and mustard spilled here and there and a few broken glasses and plates wouldn't trouble her in the least.

Otto was at work that morning, so the four of us set about making the biggest mess of his house as we could. No room was safe from our inventiveness. After we emptied the contents of the refrigerator and kitchen cabinets onto the floor, shaving cream and toothpaste tubes were squished around in the bathrooms. Clothes were taken out of the bedroom closets and even the shades on the windows weren't safe from us. They got unwound and landed on the floors.

It was the only bad example my mother ever taught my brother and sister and me, but it also was one of the most fun things I ever did.

The summer of 1941, after having spent only a year away for a side trip to a West Side world that was more luxurious but one we hadn't liked at all, we were back in our element. We were back home in the old Polish neighborhood around Division Street and Milwaukee and Ashland Avenues. The flat was only a few blocks from the one we had lived in on Bosworth Avenue, but we came to like Marshfield better than any street we ever lived on.

There was always a routine about our moving. My father got some of his friends from the bus lines to rent a truck and helped load it with our things. After arriving at the new flat, while they unloaded the truck, Mom gave us kids show money and told us to stay for two pictures.

We went around the corner on Division to the Crown and saw "Blossoms in the Dust," with Greer Garson as a pioneering lady who started an orphanage, and "Boom Town," with Clark Gable and Spencer Tracy playing friends who drilled for oil. They were both great and are considered classics today.

When we got back to the apartment, Mom had fried chicken and French fries for us. The movers had gone and everything was put where she wanted it. We were home.

We lived in that apartment the longest, for seven years, while we kids finished grammar and high school. It was a big six-room, three bedroom apartment with a long hallway through the middle, separating the rooms, on the second floor of a brick two-story. A candy store was at the front of the first floor facing the street, and a smaller apartment was behind that where an Irish policeman and his wife who owned the store lived with their little boy and girl.

It was like heaven living above a candy store and ice cream parlor. We kids would scrape together some nickels on hot summer days and buy ice cream and soda downstairs. Sis and I bought movie magazines on sale there each month and kept up with what new movies would be showing at the Crown and Biltmore, the two fanciest theaters within walking distance. Johnny bought comic books. They cost only a nickel or a dime and Superman and Batman had become very popular.

A grocery store was on one corner up the block and a tavern across the street from it. Dad spent a lot more time in the tavern than he did in the grocery store.

Mom would send us to shop at the store and the grocer let us open a charge account. Most of the time we bought what we wanted "on the cuff" and Mom paid the grocer at the end of the week, if she had the money. "On the cuff" was a term that referred back to a store owner's habit of marking onto the cuff of his shirtsleeve what a customer owed him. He'd need a big cuff to keep track of what we owed.

It was always an adventure to bring back home what Mom wanted from the grocery store. Once she told me to buy "a pound and a half of meatless beef." The butcher finally figured she must mean ground beef.

Another time, she gave me a grocery list and after I'd gotten the items off the shelves that she wanted and went to the butcher's counter, I read from her list and asked him for some "bologna." He looked at me as if I was a Martian and scratched his head. "What?" he asked. I repeated, "bo-log-na!" It took him a while, until dawn seemed to break in his head and he said, "Oh, you want some *boloney* sausage!" Mom had spelled it right, and I pronounced it the way it was spelled. Why was the laugh on me?

It was like living next to a farm, because every Saturday morning the grocer hauled out crates of live chickens, ducks, and geese and put them out in front on his sidewalk. Neighborhood mothers and grandmothers came out in their aprons and house slippers and picked out a choice live bird. The butcher would kill it for them.

If Mom wanted to make Polish *czarnina* or "blood soup," a murky, sour combination of duck's or goose's blood, vinegar, pork neck bones, prunes and prune juice, raisins, carrots, and onions, the grocer drained the bird's blood and gave it to us in a pint jar.

Mom made the soup every now and then, especially for holiday dinners, and Dad and Johnny and Sis loved it. I hated it, so she made a little clear broth for me.

Since, as always, nothing went to waste, the duck's or goose's feathers were plucked and kept. When cleaned and dried, they were saved until enough was gathered to be made into soft, warm, "featherbed" quilts. The goose down quilts were light yet very warm to sleep under on cold winter nights. They've become very popular today.

I never had a featherbed quilt to sleep under. Everyone else at home got one or two blankets but I only got one. For added warmth, I put my winter jacket, the collar up around my shoulders. Others in the house added their coats on top of me so that when I woke up the next morning, I was warm but worn out under the weight of them all. The fire in the coal stove in the kitchen usually went out overnight. When I woke up the next morning, my nose would be cold.

Dad got up first and made a fire so that by the time Mom and the rest of us got up, at least the kitchen would be warm.

Johnny went to Wells High School a few blocks west on Augusta Boulevard, while Mary Jane and I went to Anderson Elementary School a mile or more away. There were no school buses in those days. We walked to school every morning, rain, snow, below-zero, or sunshine.

One winter morning I didn't wear a hat or mittens for the long walk to school because I thought they made me look like a sissy. It was subzero out and by the time I got to school, I was nearly frozen. I hung up my jacket in the cloak room of my "home room" and sat down at my seat, which was next to a radiator. The warmth felt good until, after only a few minutes, my hands began to tingle. Soon they began to feel as if needles were sticking into them and I couldn't help it. I got up and told my home room teacher, a tall, big woman named Mrs. Jensen who taught history.

Mrs. Jensen could tell my hands had gotten frost-bitten. She rushed me to a fountain in the hall and had me put my hands under the cold water while she rubbed them. Before long they were okay again.

I liked the school and teachers and kids there a lot. I especially liked the English class because we read stories and got to write essays. I also liked an art class because we learned to carve things out of bars of soap.

I hated gym because I was such a klutz. I was always the last one picked for any relay team. Nobody wanted me on a basketball team because if I got the ball, I never knew which way to run with it.

I made lots of friends at school, but we lived about the farthest away from it. None of the kids I was in class with lived anywhere near me, so we never became good friends.

Not long after I started school there, one of my classmates, a bully named Hank who had a long Polish last name and was twice my size, began picking on me. I was eleven and a talker, not a fighter. My mother said I was a peace-loving kind of kid, like her brother Martin. He always had tried talking an adversary out of fighting, and I used the same approach.

I was afraid then, that all through grammar school and high school, some bully would come up and make trouble and I'd have to fight him or get beaten up. I hated the thought of facing battles like that every day for years to come.

One afternoon, Hank came up and stood toe-to-toe in front of me in the schoolyard at recess.

"Okay, let's see if you're too scared to fight," he said, challenging me in front of all my classmates.

He put up his dukes and got into a fight position and I knew the time had come. I wouldn't be able to talk my way out of this fight.

I raised my fists to defend myself and Hank lunged at me, landing a hard fist to my chin. I staggered back and some of my classmates caught me, then pushed me right back at the bully. I don't know where it came from, but I got the nerve to fight him back on his own terms.

I wasn't very good at it, but some of my arm-flailing hit their marks and my fists landed on Hank a couple of times. After we exchanged a few more blows, he stepped back and dropped his mitts. Then he reached out and put a hand on my shoulder.

"Okay," he said. "I just wanted to see if you'd fight back."

Hank and I became friends after that and, to my relief, it was the only time I had to fight anyone at school.

Another day, in English class, I was busy writing an essay with pen and ink, dipping the pen every so often in the ink in the inkwell at the top right corner of the desk, when a visitor came to the classroom. She was a nice gray-haired woman who was a teacher at another school and was with a group touring English classes in schools around the city.

Our teacher told us to just keep on with our essays. While I went back to writing mine, the woman stopped beside my desk and looked down at my paper. My name was at the top.

"Your last name is the same as mine," the woman said, surprised. "What is your father's first name?"

I told her and she smiled.

"Then I'm your Aunt Helen!" she said.

It was Dad's cousin who had heard a ghost's footsteps when her mother died.

Aunt Helen was one of the nicest, kindest, and also the smartest people I ever met. Several years later the family visited her at her house and she played the piano for us, beautifully. She devoted her life to teaching Chicago school children and years later at this writing is 94 and blind, living in a nursing home.

I thought Aunt Helen was rich, her house was so nice. Actually it was just a very nice upper middle-class home.

I had the same mistaken notion about one of my class-mates. I thought a handsome, black curly-haired boy named Marvin was rich because one real cold winter day after school he invited me to his house. Actually it was an apartment, in a four-story brick building a few blocks from the school. But we had never lived in apartment buildings, just the second floor of old two-story houses.

Marvin's building had a hallway where the mail boxes were located on a wall, and the stairs were nicely carpeted. His folks had nice furniture and lamps and things but what impressed me the most was the bathroom. On the wall beside the mirror and medicine cabinet was something I had never seen before. I asked him what it was and he showed me. Our hands were red and chapped from the cold weather, and he pressed a little button over a container that started some white stuff like toothpaste pouring out. He rubbed it over his hands and they began to look oily, smelling sweet and nice.

It was a lotion dispenser with Hinds Honey and Almond Cream. I tried it and wished we had one like it in our bathroom. But I knew that was impossible. Only rich kids, like Marvin, lived with luxuries like that.

There were things like that to be found in the five-and-ten-cent store up on Milwaukee Avenue a few blocks from our apartment. My brother and sister and I went there after school or on Saturdays to see what the hawkers were trying to sell next. Fast-talking salesmen in striped silk shirts and shiny suits sold the darndest stuff at a special counter set up in front of the store. One week a man demonstrated how great some knives cut. The next week, another man touted the many virtues and uses of a new cough syrup.

Johnny, who had seen even more movies than Sis or I and had picked up a lot more general knowledge that way, said the hawkers were modern-day versions of the old snake oil sales-men who traveled the country in medicine shows and carnivals.

Mary Jane and I stood with our mouths open in front of the hawker's counter and watched the demonstrations. The one that was the most exciting was a salesman who shouted the praises of an anti-itch powder. His sales pitch went on and on as he got more excited by the minute, telling how the powder could cure even the worst case of athlete's foot. He even said it cured a man whose feet itched so much, they had to strap him down on a table or he'd have gone crazy.

We never bought any of the things the hawkers promoted. They cost a dollar or more and we only had a dime or two to spend. We spent our money on candy and just browsed around the store. Sis might buy some new cut-outs for her paper doll collection, and Johnny and I might buy a new yo-yo or some caps for our cap pistols.

At home, after school, we kids had homework or chores to do before we could go out and play.

Mary was the most studious of the three of us, but homework never took much of her after-school time. She would, however, spend hours curled up in the stuffed chair in the parlor, reading story books.

We never had a dog or cat or even a canary. Maybe it was because keeping a pet cost too much to feed. One day Mom brought home a fishbowl and three goldfish. She named them after the Andrews Sisters, popular vocalists of the day.

After only about a week, one evening she said she had bad news for us kids:

"There's been a death in the family," Mom announced gravely.

We kids wondered what aunt or uncle had died, then Mom told us,

"Patty died today."

One of the Andrews Sisters goldfish had gone to that big fishbowl in the sky. It wasn't long before Maxine and Lavergne joined her. That was the end of any pets in our house.

We kids didn't have much spare money for pets, ourselves. But Mom gave us each a dime allowance at the end of the week for doing chores around the house.

Mary's chore was to get dinner ready for us. She either heated up what Mom had prepared that morning before leaving for work at the telephone company or followed instructions for a recipe Mom left for her.

In summer, Johnny and I took turns taking the garbage to the alley each day after school. In winter, I took out the garbage and his job was to take out the ashes from the coal stove. We took turns each day making sure the two coal buckets were full of coal.

Emptying the garbage and ashes and getting the coal required a trip down the long flight of wooden stairs that zig-zagged across the back of the building. Below the stairs and down a few steps from the back yard was a shed where the coal was delivered and stored.

I was always scared to go down for the coal, afraid the boogie man would get me. When it was my turn after school to go down and shovel the coal, I did it as fast as I could.

It would be dark after school on gray winter afternoons, or for some reason I had to wait until night to do the chore and it would be darker still. I took the buckets and a pack of matches and left the kitchen, went down the back stairs, and set the buckets down outside the shed. After unlocking the shed door, I opened it and immediately rats and spiders inside began scurrying around for cover. Pushing cobwebs from over the door that clung to my face, I was lucky if a spider didn't run down my neck or a rat didn't run up my pants leg.

Quickly as I could, I lit a candle that was kept propped up on the coal pile, so I could see to shovel. Fast as I could, I shoveled coal into the two buckets. Then I took them outside, blew out the candle, and locked the shed door. Afterward I ran up the stairs with a filled coal bucket in each hand.

I wouldn't feel safe from the boogie man until I got the buckets inside the kitchen and locked the latch on the back door. Then I breathed a sigh of relief and wondered how I could do it again and escape the boogie man, when I had to get coal again in a day or two.

Worrying about a boogie man getting me, which started when I was eleven on those coal-shoveling excursions into the dark world of the backyard and shed at night, may have come from two other events that year.

The first was, that summer the news on the radio was that an ax murderer was on the loose in Chicago. Parents were cautioned to keep their children off the streets after school. Mom kept us home after school while a police manhunt went on for the ax-killer, but took a further precaution. She kept a big pot of water boiling on the kitchen stove at all times, refilling it as it evaporated into steam. Her strategy would be, if the ax-killer came to our street and tried to open the entrance door to our hallway below and next to the candy store, she would open the window right above the door and pour scalding water on his head.

She must have gotten the idea for that trick by seeing Charles Laughton in "The Hunchback of Notre Dame," when he was high up in the bell tower of the cathedral. He began pouring hot water down on the heads of an angry mob trying to get him.

Fortunately, the ax murderer was found after a few days and Mom didn't have to put her plan into action.

Maybe the ax murderer scared me and I began thinking of him as the boogie man. Or else, it was someone else...

One afternoon our class at school went on a field trip, walking about a mile to a Polish museum in the neighborhood.

It was interesting to see the memorabilia there, but then I saw someone who frightened me. A man I saw there had only half a face. The right side was normal, but the left side seemed blank. He had no ear on that side and only half a nose. Compared to him, Freddie in "Nightmare on Elm Street" is positively good-looking.

I began seeing the man in our neighborhood after that. I didn't want to, because I felt sorry for him, but I always had to look away. The strange thing is, over the years I've seen the same man, in various parts of the city where I've lived.

He must be eighty, but that could be. He might have only been twenty when I first saw him.

I've wondered how his face got that way. Had he been in one of the wars and gotten injured in a bomb explosion? Had he become the victim of poison gas? Surely he couldn't have been in World War I, but maybe he was just an infant or boy in Europe when World War II began. He might have gotten his injury there.

Maybe neither of those men was my boogie man. I'd certainly seen enough scary movies to frighten me, such as Boris Karloff as Frankenstein and Bela Lugosi as Count Dracula. Maybe they crept into my dreams and turned them into nightmares that someone was after me when I went down for the coal.

In the nightmares, I ran up the stairs after getting the coal, but dropped the buckets on the porch outside the kitchen door, then rushed inside. But before I could slide the latch on the door, I saw the boogie man looking in through the window of the door. The door started to open. Then I would wake up, just before the boogie man could get me.

Doing the after-school chores sometimes led to disputes between Johnny and me. One day when I was about to take out the garbage, he told me,

"While you're going to the alley, take the ashes with you."

"That's *your* job!" I reminded him.

"Take the ashes with you," he said sternly, "or I'll break Mom's new broom over your back."

"You wouldn't dare!" I shouted.

After he broke the broom over my back, I lifted up a green-painted wooden ash-tray stand that stood about knee-high in the parlor. I broke it over the back of his left leg.

Johnny was ready to just about kill me. Instead, he calmed down and didn't lay a hand on me.

"Mom'll be home from work in half an hour," he said. "We'd better repair the damage."

While I went to the grocery store and bought a new broom "on the cuff," Johnny got some bandage tape. He wrapped it around one of the legs of the ash-tray stand, then painted the repair job green with some water colors from our school supplies.

Just after he finished and I got back from the store and put the new broom in its proper corner in the kitchen, Mom came home. First thing she did when she came home after work each day was survey the apartment to see what damage we had done.

Mom had eyes like a hawk. It only took her a minute to spot the changes.

"What happened to the other broom? That's a brand-new one. And how did the ash-tray stand get broken? What have you wild men been up to today?"

Johnny and I each caused our share of the battles and damage, but Mary Jane was no slouch and may even have edged my brother and me out a little.

My brother got so mad at my sister at times, when our folks were at work, he went after her and she ran and hid in the bathroom, locking the door after her. One day Johnny got so mad at Mary Jane and then so frustrated when she locked herself in the bathroom, he tore the door right off its hinges. Sis stood cowering in the bathtub, pleading, "Don't hit me!"

"It's okay, Sis," he replied, backing off. "I won't hit you. I got the anger out of me by tearing the door down. Now I'd better re-hang it, before Mom comes home."

My sister and I often fought like two cats on a fence at night, but it was because we palled together so much, going to the show or playing. Johnny was almost four years older and hung out with friends his own age. Since we moved so often and had few friends of our own, Sis and I spent a lot of time together.

After a fight, she and I would always make up real fast. It was because Mom always told us, "Never let the sun set on an argument. Always make up, right away."

Even after a skirmish with Sis, some nights when there would be a loud thunderstorm, she came into my room and sat on my bed, even if I was asleep, but wouldn't wake me up.

Every Saturday, Mary Jane and I had other chores while Johnny would be out earning dimes running errands for neighbors. Sis and I swept and dusted the apartment and she did the dishes while I scrubbed the kitchen floor.

On Saturday afternoon we hung the laundry. Some families had home ringer-type washing machines, but we didn't. These also were the days before clothes dryers.

Each week our clothes were sent out to be washed at a commercial laundry. Having them also dried and folded cost more money than we could afford, so our laundry was returned as "wet wash" that needed drying.

If it was summer, we hung the clothes on a line that extended outside our pantry window to the second floor of the apartment next door. We hung the clothes on the line with clothes pins, then worked a pulley that moved the line across to the other end.

In winter, we strung clothesline in the kitchen, from the radiator to the hall doorway and back to the outside door, then across again until we had about six rows of line. All day and sometimes into the evening the clothes dried on the line and we had to stoop under sheets and towels to get to the sink or the stove or ice box. Eventually the clothes dried, from the heat of the coal stove, and we sorted, folded, and put them away. Mom and Sis ironed whatever needed pressing, such as sheets, pillow cases, handkerchiefs, shirts and blouses.

While we cleaned house and did the laundry we listened to our favorite Saturday radio shows, starting with "Let's Pretend" in which a different fairy tale was dramatized for a half hour each week. Another favorite those mornings was "Grand Central Station," which told a different dramatic story about the life of some people whose lives at one point intertwined at the station, "crossroads of a million private lives."

I loved the stories we heard over the radio. My imagination had a field day and I pictured myself being the main character in each story.

I was eleven then and began to write my own stories. I never showed them to anyone, but they were another way I found to live outside the house. I wrote westerns and gangster stories but never love stories. I didn't know much about love, and still hadn't had a girlfriend. The reason for that was probably because I was shy.

If Johnny had a girlfriend or a whole pile of them, I never knew. He never talked about girls. He was about fourteen then and I just had a hunch he had learned to smoke cigarettes and probably had learned about girls, too.

How he'd learned about girls, I couldn't guess, because neither Mom nor Dad told him or me about them, the way Lewis Stone did as "Judge Hardy" in the movies, telling his teenaged boy Andy, played by Mickey Rooney, about the birds and the bees.

To me, birds and bees were just birds and bees. Yet I had a sneaking hunch my older brother knew they did something that had to do with "making out."

In grammar school, none of the teachers taught us about the birds or bees either. The only thing about our bodies they taught us was to brush our teeth. They did that by showing black and white classroom movies of giant-sized molars with arms and legs, tap-dancing around with humongous tooth brushes. That was about as close to sex education as schools came in the early 1940s.

I figured I had a long way to go before I was going to learn about girls, but was still in no hurry. Johnny didn't seem to be in any hurry either, because when he wasn't out playing with his pals or running errands, he built model airplanes out of balsa wood, tissue paper, and glue. He had a mechanical drawing board on a table in the bedroom we shared with bunk beds, and spent hours cutting out the wings and fuselage and other parts from sheets of balsa wood.

After he built a single or double-winged plane that might have taken weeks to put together, he took it outside in the nearest empty lot. He would wind up the propeller with a rubber band and let the plane go.

A whole bunch of us kids would watch expectantly and Johnny's planes never disappointed us. They flew high over our heads and circled around, then came down for a landing. Most of the time, instead of landing, they nose-dived and crashed. The delicate wood and tissue would be broken or torn. Johnny would pick up the wreckage of the plane and take it back home. He would work for more hours or days repairing it so it could fly again. It always seemed a lot of work for such a short flight, but my brother was always willing to spend the time at it.

He always built his model planes alone, but sometimes let me help him build something with his Erector set. I loved using a little screw driver on the tiny nuts and screws that held the pieces of metal together with which he built cars, trucks, houses, even skyscrapers.

One day Dad brought home a little motor that worked with the Erector set and helped Johnny and me build a Ferris wheel. It actually went around, with seats for toy people to sit in, and I thought it was the neatest thing I'd ever seen.

That summer we went to the Crown and saw Judy Garland as Dorothy in "The Wizard of Oz." She'd left the drab farm she had lived on and went somewhere "over the rainbow" to a beautiful land where she had great adventure.

Mary Jane and I wished we could go somewhere like that, while we did our Saturday chores. Sis washed and dried the dishes and cleaned the kitchen and bathroom while I scrubbed the kitchen floor.

The closest I came to being Over the Rainbow was one day when we were blowing soap bubbles out front of the candy store.

Dad smoked a pipe then. We took two of his favorites and dipped them into a soap bubble mixture of water and bar soap. We must have ruined the pipes for him, but he never mentioned it to us.

One bubble I blew that sunny day grew big and round and I saw a rainbow reflected in it. I held my breath, in awe at the beauty of the colors in that rainbow, and wished it would stay there forever. But, as all bubbles do, it burst. The wet soap water splashed in my face and I came back down from over the rainbow to Marshfield Avenue.

I began trying to see that rainbow again, or something as beautiful as it.

Chapter Thirteen

Oh! we ain't got a barrel of money,
Maybe we're ragged and funny,
But we'll travel along, singing a song,
Side by side.

The summer of 1941 was especially hot. There was only a small electric fan on top the ice box in the kitchen to blow a cooling breeze. Some days, Mom gave us each a dime and my brother and sister and I went to North Avenue Beach for a swim in the lake.

Our problem was, how to spend our dime. It cost five cents to take a couple of streetcars to the beach, which was several miles away and took at least an hour to get to. A dime would get us rides to and from the beach, but when we got there, we always wished we had an ice cream cone. So our dilemma was, if we spent a nickel on a cone, should we walk to the beach or back from it? The walk would take about two hours, but we'd rather walk one way than not have the ice cream cone.

Usually we took the street car to the beach and spent the day there. We bought ice cream cones when we were leaving and licked them on the way walking back home.

One night when we got back from our long walk home from the beach, it was as hot or hotter than when we left that morning. Mom and Dad were both out, working, so we kids were home alone. Johnny looked at me and shook his head, frowning.

"You've got a bad sunburn. The best thing to do is go right to bed. Don't drink any water, and cover yourself with a couple of blankets."

Trustingly, I did what my big brother suggested. When I was in bed with two blankets on me, he came in and shut the window in my bedroom. "Better not get any fresh air," he cautioned, then left and closed the door.

I felt like a hot dog sizzling in a frying pan, but stayed in bed. I tried to sleep, but could hardly even breathe in that hot, stuffy room with no air coming into it.

Some time later, the folks came home and Mom looked in on me. Thank heavens she did, or by morning I might have been what Uncle Stash called a *"poshkudny* case!"

"Wally, you look like you're on fire!" Mom gasped. "Why is your window closed? Why do you have all those blankets on you?"

Dad gave it to Johnny for that.

The city was so hot that summer, even the folks talked about some way to get away from it for a few days. We still didn't have a car and never went on vacation. But one weekend we took the train down to Springfield and visited Mom's sister, our Aunt Julia, and her husband and family. They had a house across a road from her mother-in-law who had a small chicken farm.

That Sunday while we were getting ready to leave and return to Chicago, Aunt Julia invited us kids to stay for a week. It sounded good because I never had been on a farm of any kind before.

The first night after my folks and brother and sister left, I stood on the front porch looking up at all the stars in the sky. I hadn't seen a sky like it before, because the lights of Chicago were too bright to show a star-filled sky. I caught a bad case of homesickness that night. But the worst was yet to come, and it was another kind of sickness.

At breakfast the next morning with my cousins, Aunt Julia poured us all glasses of milk. I liked milk, until I tasted what she gave me. I didn't know milk tasted so sweet and sour at the same time and as awful as that. When she saw my face, she explained, "It's goat's milk, from goats on the farm across the road."

I swallowed the goat's milk fast, so I could hardly taste it. To be polite, I pretended I liked it, but didn't ask for seconds.

The following morning I tried pretending I was sleeping late, hoping my cousins would drink all the goat's milk. No luck. I heard Aunt Julia tell her kids, "Be sure to save some goat's milk for Wally. You know how much he likes it!"

Brother Johnny was a late sleeper, so he usually slept through breakfast and escaped any chance of being served Aunt Julia's favorite elixir. Sis Mary said she ran out the back door every morning, for fear of being served any of it.

One evening, Aunt Julia said she had a "Very special treat" for us visiting kids. "Goat's milk ice cream!"

We were trapped. If you can imagine what frozen Yak's milk might taste like, goat's milk must come close.

Before we leave Aunt Julia, a few words about her daughter, Betty. Some women have a thing about horses. Betty had a thing about apes, especially one of the biggest of them all, who resided in a cage at the Lincoln Park Zoo in Chicago. Bushman was world-famous for being one of the biggest gorillas in captivity.

Betty, after her teenage years and into her young twenties when she was a medium-sized young dark-haired woman, made it a part of her annual vacation plans to visit the Lincoln Park Zoo's star attraction. She never gave us much advance warning that she was coming, as if the telephone lines never had been strung between Springfield and Chicago. To Betty, the lines only worked between the Greyhound bus station in Chicago and our house.

Bushman was a 550-pound giant gorilla, world-famous for being one of the largest apes in captivity. Betty simply loved him, but she wasn't alone. The whole world loved him.

Bushman had been orphaned as an infant and came to the zoo in Chicago in 1930, the same year I was born. I didn't get to meet him until I was about four or five, but Betty who was several years older than I, saw him a few years before I did.

The nation's zoo directors voted Bushman "the most outstanding animal in any zoo in the world and the most valuable." He may even have inspired the motion picture *King Kong*, which first startled movie audiences in 1933 and remains one of the great thrillers of the movies.

Bushman had been abandoned in the jungles of Cameroon in West Africa and sold to the Lincoln Park Zoo for $3,500 by a Presbyterian missionary and an animal trader. One writer said Bushman was "like a nightmare that escaped from darkness into daylight. His hand is the kind of thing a sleeper sees reaching for him just before he wakes up screaming."

Bushman was not a very social animal. He was known to throw his food and even his dung at photographers. Those who had been pelted claimed his aim was more accurate than any pitcher for the Chicago Cubs or White Sox.

Cousin Betty was among thousands who flocked to the zoo to see Bushman each year.

My favorite author, F. Scott Fitzgerald, wrote that "In a real dark night of the soul, it is always three o'clock in the morning."

Betty's gorilla call sometimes came to us an hour earlier. She would phone us or Aunt Mary as early at two o'clock in the morning to say she was at a downtown bus station and in town to see Bushman.

One day in June, 1950, about 120,000 people came to see Bushman when he was ill and they feared he might be dying. But he survived, and in October escaped from his cage through an accidentally unlocked door. He roamed the zoo's kitchen and corridors for nearly three hours. An army of zoo guards and police couldn't capture him, but a garter snake scared him into going back into his cage.

Bushman died on New Year's Day in 1951. For many weeks, his mourning fans filed past his cage. Betty came up for a final farewell. The big ape's mounted remains are on display today at Chicago's Field Museum of Natural History.

Perhaps to take her mind off her loss when Bushman died, Cousin Betty joined the U.S. Navy.

Not long after I got back home from visiting Aunt Julia's goat's milk paradise in Springfield, Johnny hanged himself.

One night, just before Mom was expected home from work, he rigged a rope up above the door in the dining room. Standing on a chair just inside the room, he tied a noose around his neck.

When my mother came up the stairs, she opened the door and saw her eldest son hanging by his neck. She nearly had a heart attack, not knowing Johnny was only fooling. He was holding on to the rope with one hand.

Johnny got it for that, too.

Why did my brother do such things? I didn't try to figure it out at the time, but maybe it was his way of blowing off steam because not long after our parents remarried, they started quarreling again. Dad went back to his old ways of drinking and gambling. Nothing much seemed to have changed. He still didn't come home with his pay on any regular basis and the bills began piling up again.

Johnny began running away about then. He didn't want to stay home and listen to the arguments between our folks, so he skipped school and disappeared until long after dark. Then he came home reluctantly, only because he was sleepy or hungry.

Mary and I were a few years younger and didn't have the courage to run away. We stayed home and listened to the arguments or found show money and escaped to one of the neighborhood movie theaters.

Sometimes, my sister stayed home and finished reading a book instead of going to the movies with Johnny and me. She read and reread all the Louisa May Alcott books such as *Little Women* and *Little Men*, and another favorite, *Peter and Katrinka*, about a brother and sister in Holland.

Years later, Sis told me that those books she liked reading most were stories of happy family life. She read them as escape literature because our own homelike wasn't very happy.

None of the three of us was able to make friends we could keep for very long, because we moved so much, so movies and books were the best substitutes we could find for friends. Since my brother was older and stayed away from home so much, my sister and I became close friends, like Peter and Katrinka.

Cold weather came on. We had an early snowfall after Thanksgiving. One night, when we told Mom that a rerun of Shirley Temple in "Heidi" was showing at one of the theaters, she said we should all go. It was a picture about living in a Swiss village and the Alps. Mom loved mountains and missed the ones where she'd grown up.

Johnny was working at the bowling alley, so Dad, Mom, Sis and I went to see "Heidi" which ran with another feature at the Oakley theater on Chicago Avenue, about six miles from where we lived. It was near zero out and we walked, to save the street car fare. Snow that fell a few days earlier crunched under our shoes. We had never walked that far in such cold weather to see a movie.

Several times along the way, as we passed a tavern, Dad made a stop. He went in and had a shot of whiskey while we waited outside. After a while, Dad came out again and we continued on our way.

Each time I looked in to see Dad, he was sitting alone at the bar. I wondered if he sat alone in taverns on the nights he stayed away from home, after gambling away his pay. Did he prefer drinking alone at bars to being home with us? It was something I still couldn't figure out.

Finally we got to the theater and saw "Heidi" and another picture. By the time they were over and the lights went on and the theater was closing, it was past midnight. The walk home that frozen night seemed even longer, and Dad was silent. All the taverns had closed.

We kids had hot chocolate when we got home early that morning and Mom fixed some hot tea for her and Dad.

My mother usually had a pan on top the coal stove in the evening, boiling water for coffee or tea. One night when Dad came home from work he was cold and thought a cup of hot tea would be good. Mom was somewhere else in the house when he came home, so he helped himself. He saw a pan steaming on the stove and it looked like some tea Mom was keeping warm. He poured a cupful of what was in the pot and took a good swallow, then spat it out and yelled, holding his throat.

"What's in that pan?" he cried.

Mom came rushing into the kitchen and realized what had happened.

"That was hot lard I was rendering!" she explained.

Dad considered himself lucky. He hadn't burned his throat out, just scorched it a little.

He didn't fare as well not long after that. One rainy night driving a trolley on the Northwest Side of the city, a friend driving ahead of him had a minor accident. The trolley came off the track overhead and the man got out to work some pulleys to get it back onto the electric line.

My father had a premonition something bad might happen. He was right. The motorman didn't have rubber boots on and stood in the wet street while he tried getting the trolley back on the track. A high voltage of electricity shot through him and the man got such a shock, he couldn't let go of the end of the trolley line he held.

Dad stopped his bus and ran to help the man, but he didn't have rubber boots on, either. It didn't matter. He tackled his friend and the force made the man release his grip so he was freed of the electricity. But in making contact with the man, the same voltage went through Dad. Miraculously, neither was killed or hurt badly, but for the rest of his life, Dad had a high-pitched ringing in his ears.

We never knew it bothered him, because he never mentioned it. He always looked relaxed and peaceful those nights at home, reading the next day's newspaper. But a constant ringing in the ears can drive anyone almost batty. He just learned to live with it.

The weekend poker parties at Grandma's and Grandpa's house on the South Side continued several times a month. Mom began wearing a red blouse to them, for luck. It usually didn't help.

Grandma Kate, a big and heavy-set old woman by then, had been sick for years. When she could no longer walk, she got around the house in a wheelchair. But by that winter, she couldn't get out of bed.

After work and taking care of Dad and us kids, Mom took a streetcar out to see Grandma, to help her as often as she could. She bathed the old woman and washed and set her hair.

For nearly twenty years, Grandma disliked Mom because she married her first son. On one of those visits Mom made after work to help her, Grandma finally thanked her for all her kindness and asked to be forgiven. Mom didn't make a big thing out of it. She was just glad they finally were on good terms.

A tall old wooden clock stood on a shelf on the kitchen wall, just outside Grandma's bedroom. It was a thirty-day wind-up clock, but no one ever remembered winding it. It just kept running, tick-tocking and sounding a lovely chime on the quarter, half, and hour. One morning, the clock stopped, the moment Grandma died.

She was waked at Ketchum's funeral parlor and we kids all thought that name was funny.

After the funeral most of the family returned from the cemetery to Grandma's house where drinks and food were served in the kitchen. Later, Dad and his brothers and sisters and we children all left the kitchen, gathering in the parlor with Grandpa. After a few minutes, a loud crash startled everyone. It came from the kitchen, sounding as if pots and pans had fallen and glasses and dishes had crashed to the floor and broke.

Everyone ran through the dining room and looked into the kitchen, but there was no sign of anything having fallen. No pots or pans were on the floor. All the glasses and plates were still in their cabinets.

Two aunts checked out the pantry just off the kitchen. They reported that nothing had fallen or was broken there, either.

Everyone agreed, however. We all heard the deafening crash of pans falling and glass breaking in the kitchen.

What had caused the noise? We never knew.

Another event took place that December that shook more than Grandma's house. The Japanese launched a surprise attack on Pearl Harbor in Hawaii on Sunday, December 7. The next day, we were at war.

Chapter Fourteen

Bless 'em all, Bless 'em all,
The long and the short and the tall

Newspapers, radio, and movie newsreels were full of stories about how bad things were in the Pacific and Europe. When World War II started in 1941 when I was eleven, the first impression I got of it was not from the media but from bubble gum cards. I could no longer find "Cowboys and Indians" cards. Instead of cavalrymen lying on a bloody battlefield with Indian arrows stuck in them, the bubble gum cards showed atrocity scenes. G.I.s lay on the ground with Jap bayonets in them or were being shot by Nazi storm troopers. The amount of blood was about the same as in the Cowboy and Indian cards and we learned to hate the symbols of the rising sun and the swastika.

Every dime I got for chores or running errands, I ran to the five-and-ten-cent store and bought another lead soldier, adding it to a new collection I started. For a dime I bought a soldier with his rifle, either kneeling, standing, or on his stomach firing off a round, or a G.I. in position to throw a hand grenade. For fifteen cents there were howitzers and cannons on wheels, and a quarter bought trucks, tanks, and ambulances. A boy on the block collected them too and we got together after school to play war on the sidewalk.

Sometimes Mary and I spent our dimes on war stamps, because we didn't have enough money to buy war bonds. A certain number of stamps or bonds paid for a rifle or bomb or tank. Oh, yes, when my sister started high school, we dropped the Jane from Mary Jane.

The following spring, rationing began. Americans by the thousands went to their local schools to receive their War Ration Book. Every American was limited to one pound of sugar every two weeks and 25 to 30 gallons of gasoline per motorist per month.

Rationing began in 1942, after a year into the war. President Roosevelt asked it of us and we would do anything to win the war. We also would do anything for him. On almost every American kitchen wall, including ours, were two pictures: a photograph of FDR and a painting of Jesus we got from the Salvation Army or the YMCA. When FDR died during his fourth term as President in 1945, it was like everyone lost a member of the family. And not only a member, but the head of the family.

Before long, meat also was rationed. Besides needing the money to buy it, shoppers had to have the rationing stamps to permit them to buy the limit of 28 ounces of meat per week per adult.

To further conserve meat, Americans later were asked to refrain from eating meat on Tuesdays and poultry on Thursdays, to help stockpile grain for starving people in Europe.

Meatless Tuesdays and poultry-less Thursdays were observed religiously in our home. We Catholics were used to not eating meat on Fridays. Now we had to learn to like fish on two days of the week. Some people grew to hate fish, but not me. I still eat it twice a week.

My mother and aunts began swapping ration coupons with each other and neighbors, if they needed food staples but didn't have the required coupons. Shoppers were only allowed four ounces of butter a week, four pounds of cheese, and coffee and flour also were rationed.

Besides rationing things so more could be available to the fighting men and women in the service, everyone on the home front was asked to make what they had last longer. "Use it up, wear it out, make it do, or do without" became a familiar slogan.

Just about every consumable item was expected to have a second life, as tin and other metals, paper and nylon were recycled. Kitchen fat was saved and processed for explosives. Rubber was one of the most scarce items and tire thieves were so numerous, some cities instructed car owners to record the serial numbers of their tires. That was no problem for us because we still didn't own a car.

I felt almost like a war profiteer, getting money for the things we collected that could be recycled into useful products for the war effort. We kids went on junk hunts, collecting newspapers and magazines, rags, old tires and most anything made out of rubber, and all types of metal.

Gas stations bought used tires for a penny a pound, we could sell newspapers for 60 cents for 100 pounds, and magazines brought 80 cents for 100 pounds. Rags and iron were worth a penny a pound and aluminum and lead six cents. I always had show money, after the war started.

Every time a new battle broke out in the Pacific or Europe, the *Chicago Tribune* ran a full-page map of the area or country in color and I spent hours studying it. Then I copied the map onto typing paper and wrote in all the cities, towns, or rivers by the battle. I learned more geography doing that than I did in school. Guadalcanal, the Solomons, the Aleutians, North Africa, and Sicily became as familiar to me as places in Illinois and Indiana.

My father read the newspapers religiously and even Mom kept up with the latest news stories and who was who in FDR's administration, though we weren't always sure who she was talking about. For instance, Edward Stettinius, the U.S. Steel magnet who became priorities director. Mom called him "Ste-tin-*i*-tis." At first, we thought she was talking about an ailment instead of a politician. Same thing, I guess.

When we first went to war with Germany I thought I might be safe, if we lost and they invaded Chicago. Mom came from Austria and that was next door to Germany, so I thought maybe the Nazis would leave us alone. I began wishing we had some relative who was from Japan.

Then the war movies began playing at the theaters in our neighborhood, showing heroics of Marines in "Wake Island," the Air Force in "A Wing and a Prayer," the sailors in "Destination Tokyo," and even armed forces nurses in "So Proudly We Hail." I began to worry less. We had some pretty brave men and women fighting on our side and it looked as if we were going to win.

The war brought an end to the weekend poker parties at Grandma's house. Dad was a few years older and the father of three children so he wasn't drafted into the service, but most of his brothers were. They joined the army and were soon sent to England and, later, France.

My brother saw every war movie that came out, while he was ushering at the Biltmore and later at the Congress, farther from our neighborhood. After school, my sister and I even walked all the way to that theater. We brought Johnny a bag with his dinner, then he sneaked us in to see the double-feature showing that day.

Movies had become a favorite entertainment during the Depression, to take people's minds off the hard times. Now the war brought them to the theaters in even greater numbers. It became commonplace to see long lines outside theaters and it was nothing to wait an hour or more as some lines went around a block. Teenage ushers and usherettes in uniforms let people inside the theater in two's and showed them their seats with a flashlight, as empty seats became available. Sometimes the seats were so close to the screen we got a stiff neck looking up at it for four hours, or so far to one side of the screen, the actors looked as if they were all built skinny as Abraham Lincoln.

At home, we learned to do without some things that had been rationed or were no longer sold. Dad rolled his own cigarettes because they were rationed so the boys overseas could have them. Mom had to "paint" silk stockings on her legs because silk went to war, to make parachutes. We all had to learn to conserve on toilet paper because that was hard to get since paper was needed for the war effort.

While in seventh grade, I began working part-time after school in the candy store downstairs. My job was to bring soda bottles up from the basement and keep the cooler filled, and do any other chore the policeman or his wife gave me. I liked the work and the five dollars a week pay, but not the rats and cockroaches that inhabited the basement.

The candy store had a juke box and teenagers a few years older than me in the neighborhood began jitterbugging out front on the sidewalk or even in the street. Glenn Miller and Tommy Dorsey and all the other Big Bands and their vocalists were introducing new Hit Parade songs every week. The bobby-soxers began swooning over a skinny singer who wore a bow tie, Frank Sinatra.

There were a lot of love songs during the war, about G.I.'s missing their girls back home and their girls missing them, such as "You'd Be So Nice to Come Home To," "I'll Be Seeing You," and "Every time We Say Goodbye."

Since World War Two, some wars have been so short, writers didn't even have time to write any "Miss you since you went away" songs. Other wars are too darn long and never should have started in the first place.

There also were patriotic songs during World War Two, such as "Praise the Lord and Pass the Ammunition." We kids liked the novelty songs best, such as "Gertie from Bizerte," "Mairzy Doats," and "Dig You Later -- a Hubba-Hubba-Hubba."

Little American flags began appearing in windows of the houses and apartments in our neighborhood, put there by anxious mothers. Flags had one or more stars on them, each star representing a son or daughter who had gone to war. Sometimes the star would be gold. That was for a serviceman or woman who had been killed in the war.

Besides working in the candy store and collecting things to recycle, I had another job. In its own small way I hoped it helped the war effort.

A young man who lived in an apartment next door had joined the army. He was tall and thin, dark-haired, and reminded me of Jimmy Stewart. Before being sent overseas, he married a German refugee who had come to Chicago. She was to keep the apartment and wait for him to come back when the war was over. He would send her his U.S. Army allotment wife checks.

The war bride was a pretty blonde who must have read too many 1930s movie magazines back in Germany. She wore her hair just like Jean Harlow, the platinum blonde bombshell of Hollywood in the early and mid 1930s. She also plucked her eyebrows out and penciled them in, to look like the sexy movie star. We never knew the war bride's real name, so we called her "Blondie."

Her husband's first name was Walter, but she called him Wally, only she pronounced it "Voh-lee." She promised him she would learn to write English so she could send him weekly letters while he was overseas. She didn't work; she only seemed to stay home all day and read movie magazines. This was long before television, so she only had the radio to keep her company. I don't think she dated, and was faithful to her "Voh-lee."

Because of Blondie, I got my first paid job as a writer, when I was twelve in 1942. It happened this way...

One day Blondie offered to pay me a quarter if I did her a favor. I had my eyes on a new piece of lead model field artillery at the dime store, and said sure. I thought maybe she wanted me to take out her garbage, but what she hired me to do was write a love letter she wanted to send to her Voh-lee.

I had never written a love letter to a girl, much less a man. But I could use the quarter. Besides, I hated to think her G.I. was in a trench in the mud, being shot at, but wouldn't get anything at mail call.

Blondie tried to dictate the letter, but wasn't very good at expressing her feelings in English. I thought Voh-lee deserved better, so I improvised a little. I tried to be original, but some of the lines I used came from a movie I had seen that week. Charles Boyer said the sweet nothings to Hedy Lamarr in a romance called "Algiers."

Voh-lee wrote his wife back, praising her so much for her quick command of English. Blondie hired me on a weekly basis. It was good creative writing experience for me, and I figured if the war lasted a couple more years, I'd be rich.

One day early in the war, my father and I saw battle, too. It happened when Blondie needed more help than me writing love letters to her husband. She came knocking on our door, very upset about something. Dad was home and asked what was the matter. She began talking so excitedly and fast in her poor command of English, we couldn't understand her. When she motioned for us to follow her next door, we did.

Blondie had a white angora cat whom she called "Pus-sah," which was her German-American corruption of "pussy." Soon as she opened the door to her apartment, the cat flew at us in a fright. Pussah landed on Dad's head, then ran fast as lightning down the stairs.

Dad and I wondered what scared the cat, until we looked inside Blondie's apartment. A chicken was flying around the kitchen, dripping blood on everything. A bloody knife lay on the floor.

Dad sized up the situation and told me what must have happened. Blondie had purchased a live chicken at the grocery store. In order to save money, instead of having the butcher ring its neck, she tried to kill the bird herself. She had gone after the chicken with a carving knife, but only wounded it.

Pussah returned cautiously to the apartment and watched suspiciously as Dad and I tried to catch the wounded chicken by a leg or wing. The terrified bird flapped its wings and made the most agitated sounds until finally Dad caught it. Then he did what the butcher would have done.

It was the first time Dad and I had ever worked together as a team, and we were pretty good. He rarely took my side in anything, but one day something happened that he got a chance to.

Mom had left a note before she went to work one morning that Mary and I were to buy pork chops and fry them for our dinner. She and Dad and Johnny were all out, working.

Sis figured that if she went to the grocery store and bought the chops, on the cuff of course, I ought to fry them. It was a fair division of labor and I said okay, although it would be my baptism as a chef.

The recipe my mother wrote looked easy enough. I went to the pantry and found the metal container marked "flour," put some on a plate, and covered the pork chops with some. Then I put them in a frying pan and sprinkled salt and pepper on them.

As the pork chops fried, Mary said they smelled wonderful. When they were golden brown I put them on our plates at the table, with some mashed potatoes and peas.

Sis cut a piece of her pork chop, took one bite, and spit it out.

"What have you done to it?" she asked. "It tastes so sweet!"

I tasted mine and it also tasted very sweet. I couldn't understand why, because pork chops Mom had served us never tasted sweet, and I'd followed her recipe exactly. Sis checked on it and agreed I had.

We threw the pork chops out and had corn flakes and milk for dinner. When Mom and Dad came home from work later that night we told them what had happened. Mom asked if maybe the butcher had sold us horse meat instead of pork chops, since some butchers in Chicago were reportedly doing that because of meat rationing. Sis said she bought the chops at our regular butcher and Mom was sure he'd never switch and sell us horse meat.

Something had to have been wrong with the ingredients or the recipe, Mom determined. Upon investigating, she solved the mystery. It appears that while cleaning the pantry a few days before, she mistakenly switched two significant condiments and put them in the wrong containers.

After everyone laughed at my expense, my father took my side and said anyone could have made the mistake. It wasn't my fault I had dredged the pork chops in powdered sugar instead of flour.

It was the first and last time I ever prepared candied pork chops.

I never did learn Blondie's Voh-lee's reaction when he discovered that despite his wife's faithful love-letters, she did not know how to write in English. Before he came home from the war, we had moved again.

Despite those times when we had things to laugh over, most of the time things still weren't going well at home, between my mother and father. The arguments became so frequent and upsetting, my brother began running away from home more often and staying away later at night.

My brother Johnny always had after-school and weekend jobs. First, he delivered newspapers. Without a bicycle, he used our Radio Flyer wagon to deliver the papers to homes in the neighborhood and even far beyond it where ever we lived, mostly on the North Side of Chicago. Sometimes I went with him to help.

Later, Johnny set pins in a neighborhood bowling alley, and then became an usher at the Biltmore Theater, a movie palace at Division street and Damen avenue, a few miles from where we lived in an apartment above a candy shop. My sister and I would walk there and bring his dinner in a brown paper bag and he would sneak us in to see two movies after their run in downtown Chicago.

Johnny loved the movie *They Died with Their Boots On* which showed in Chicago theaters in 1941. Errol Flynn played General George Armstrong Custer at the Little Bighorn massacre. When scenes came on in which The 7th Cavalry's marching song, *Garry Owen*, was played, Johnny would turn off his usher's flashlight, find an empty seat in the back row of the main floor, and watch the action and listen to the stirring music.

Years later, after many futile attempts to find a recording of the *Garry Owen*, I heard it on the radio, played by an army band from Louisville, Kentucky. I wrote a letter to the bandmaster asking if I could get a recording of the Irish marching song. He very graciously said that when he would take the band for its next recording session, he would have them play the Garry Owen and send me a recording.

It was a very happy day when the recording arrived by mail at our house and I surprised my brother by giving it to him. I think it was perhaps our finest moment together, as brothers.

One day in the spring of 1943 when I was thirteen and my brother was sixteen, after Mom and Dad had a particularly heated argument, Johnny left the house and didn't come back at all that night. After he stayed away two whole days and nights, Mom and Dad were worried. He was only sixteen and too young to be away from home so long.

After almost a week, the mailman delivered a post card to Mom from California. Johnny wrote that he had taken a bus to Los Angeles, on his pay from ushering and some quarters and dimes he took out of Dad's changer. He said he missed us but wanted to be on his own for a while. He would come back when Mom and Dad made up and stopped fighting, but left no address where he could be reached.

After about another week went by, Johnny phoned Mom. He said he had gotten a job selling magazines door-to-door. He had been walking on a lonely country road outside Los Angeles earlier that night when he heard a radio playing. Dinah Shore was singing "I'll Walk Alone." That did it. My brother was homesick and wanted to come home.

My mother didn't have any money to wire him. She took a streetcar that night all the way to the South Side and borrowed some money from Grandpa. Then she sent it out to Johnny in Los Angeles via Western Union. He bought a bus ticket and, a few days later, came back home.

After being home only a few weeks, my brother skipped school again and began going to movies, seeing one war picture after another. He couldn't make up his mind which he wanted to be. If he saw soldiers throwing hand grenades at a Nazi bunker in the desert, Johnny wanted to be a soldier. If the Marines were killing all the Japanese around on an island in the Pacific, he wanted to be a Marine, and so forth.

Finally, he made up his mind.

"I want to join the Navy," Johnny told Mom.

"You're too young," she protested. "You can't enlist until you're seventeen."

My mother was right. It was 1943 and young men were drafted into the service at eighteen or they could enlist at seventeen. But Johnny was still only sixteen.

My brother had a solution for that: "They'll take me if both you and Dad sign a paper giving your permission," he told her.

When my father came home that night, Mom broke the news to him. Dad also wasn't sure it was a good idea to let Johnny enlist, but my brother was determined.

169

"I'll just run away again, if you don't give your permission," Johnny said.

My mother and father knew he would. Reluctantly, they signed enlistment papers he had gotten.

"Why the Navy?" Dad asked.

"I tried the Air Force, but they said I'm color-blind," Johnny explained. "Pilots can't have trouble distinguishing colors. Then I decided I'd rather be a sailor than a soldier because on a ship, you always know where you're going to sleep and the meals are regular."

Their eldest son wasn't a kid anymore, my folks realized. Johnny had done some pretty grown-up thinking.

Before enlisting in the Navy, my brother gave me some advice.

"Don't work downstairs in the candy store much longer," he told me. "It isn't a 'real' job in the 'real' work world. Find an after-school job away from home, somewhere farther away in the neighborhood. It'll broaden your horizons and do you good."

I was thirteen then, in eighth grade at grammar school, and not quite ready yet to enter the "real" job world. I seldom did anything my brother wanted me to do anyway, so I rejected his advice. I kept my job in the candy store, all the while knowing he was right. I just hated to admit it.

We said good-bye to Johnny the day he left for the Navy and thought he looked more than ever like Ronald Reagan, the way he looked in his best movie, "King's Row." He was tall and slim and handsome and had the same boyish grin.

Johnny wrote us from where he took basic training at Great Lakes Naval Training Station north of Chicago. Later we all took the North Shore train up there one Sunday that autumn to see him graduate from "boot camp." After graduation he was assigned to the naval base at Norfolk, Virginia.

We expected him to get shipped overseas and not see him again for years. To our surprise, a few months later and a couple of days before Christmas, Johnny came home.

He had on his Navy whites, looked wonderful, and said he had gotten shore leave for the holiday. We all had a great reunion even though Mom suspected something was troubling him. He never said anything was. A few days after Christmas he told us his leave was up. He had to go back to his ship anchored at Norfolk.

The day after he left, a car pulled up outside our house. Two men in dark suits got out and rang our doorbell. My mother was home with Mary and me and we all wondered who they were. They showed identification cards and said they were F.B.I. agents. They were looking for a sailor who had jumped ship in Norfolk, and had gone A.W.O.L. (absent without leave).

Now Mom understood what had been troubling Johnny.

"My son must have just gotten homesick and wanted to come home for Christmas," she told the men. "After all, he's just sixteen. He's only a boy."

When Johnny returned to his ship, his captain saw it that way. He cautioned Johnny against ever again going A.W.O.L. because during wartime it was a crime punishable by death. But since Johnny was only sixteen and had just gone home for Christmas because he was homesick, his punishment was reduced to being confined to quarters for a week. He also would be skipped over, just once, for promotion.

My brother spent the rest of the war on an LST, a small ship that transported tanks and soldiers to battle zones in the Pacific. He ran the ship's laundry and got extra ice cream from the cook who took a liking to him. He also was the only one aboard ship besides the captain who knew how to play chess, so on many evenings, he reported to the captain's quarters and they had their own private war with knights and pawns. Johnny must have learned how to play chess on one of his adventures staying away from home before he enlisted.

After he had been in the Navy only about six months, my brother learned that his best friend in high school had joined the army and was killed. In January, 1944, George Czarny had been with the first wave of American soldiers to land on an Italian beach called Anzio.

One of my father's brothers, Leo, was in the army and stationed in England. While waiting to go across the Channel to fight the Nazis, Leo learned that another brother, Raymond, was not far away in another army unit. Leo managed to get a ride in a jeep to the other outfit and surprised him. Their letters back home told of their temporary reunion.

Mom and Sis and I took turns writing to Johnny every few days, but Dad never seemed to send him a letter. It was probably because he had nothing to write except he wished Johnny came home soon and was safe.

I wished that too. Before he left to join the Navy, I didn't think I liked my brother much. He had been pretty mean to me ever since I could remember. But one night while he was gone, I asked Mom about that. I asked her why he had been so mean.

"It was probably because Dad and I put so much responsibility onto his young shoulders, ever since he was a boy," she explained. "We asked him to look after you and Mary, while we were at work. He must have resented having to be your nursemaid and guardian, when he'd rather be off playing with his friends."

It made sense to me. Sometimes the load was too much for him.

"He may have been hard on you and Mary at times," Mom said. "But it had nothing to do with his loving you."

I began to worry then, that Johnny would get hurt or killed in the war.

Chapter Fifteen

In my arms, in my arms,
Ain't I never gonna get
a girl in my arms?

A few weeks after the Normandy Invasion on D-Day, the 6th of June, 1944, I started high school. It was good timing because just before grammar school graduation, I was in the hall changing classes with a line of other kids when my math teacher Mrs. Jordan who was the size of a sumo wrestler grabbed me by the back of my collar, looked me in the eyes, and shouted, "You talk incessantly!" The word hadn't been part of my vocabulary until then, after I looked it up in the dictionary.

We were still living above the candy store on Marshfield Avenue and for the first time, I made some friends I could keep for a while.

The neighborhood was still predominantly Polish, but Wells High School at Ashland Avenue and Augusta Boulevard a few blocks from home also was a mix of Italian, Greek, and other middle European nationalities.

My best friends in high school also lived on my block. Richard Ostrowski was short and chubby if not downright fat, and "Bonehead" Slobodka was tall and skinny. I never knew "Bonehead's" real name, but everyone called him that because he'd gotten ringworm and had all his hair shaved off. After it grew back, the name just stuck to him.

Some of the tougher guys at school smoked cigarettes on the sly, but I didn't try them mainly because of a boy named Kasimir. He was tall, thin, and dark-haired, a handsome boy who smoked cigarettes so much he smelled of them when we came near him, and his fingers were yellow.

Most of my sister's friends at school had funny names. There was Consetta Consotta and Clementine Prewitt and Tatiana Kavulchikoff and her brother Nick. Another girl's first name was Bittersweet. But two sisters on our block even beat that. Their names were Yanja and Doodoosh, and they had a little brother named TuTu.

Three pretty sisters in my classes at school were named April, May, and June. I could never make up my mind which month I liked best. Until I later met twin sisters named Eva and Veva and had a real hard time deciding between them.

One afternoon as Eva and Veva and I sat in the back of a study class while the teacher was out of the room, we began playing some kind of patty-cake game. By accident, my right hand came up under Eva's skirt and I saw her panties. She and her sister laughed, but my face turned red as a beet.

The only underpants I had seen on a female up to then didn't count. They were the gray bloomers of the old ladies when they stooped to check out the live chickens in their crates on the sidewalk at the corner grocery. Eva's were much prettier and excited me a lot more.

I didn't tell the priest my transgression that Saturday at Confession, not because it had been an accident, but because I was too embarrassed.

And I was in love again, just after starting high school, but it wasn't with a girl in class. I still liked Deanna Durbin but a new girl appeared in the movies whom I fell for hard. Jane Powell was beautiful, blonde, and also sang like an angel. I even cut class one afternoon to take a bus downtown and see and hear her on-stage at the Oriental theater.

Not much really happened in four years at Wells, maybe because they didn't have a football team and our basketball and swim teams weren't very good. I worked on the school newspaper and acted in some plays.

We had some pretty good teachers and some strange ones. One of my favorites was my English teacher, Dorothy Bailey, who was short and about as round as she was tall. She was the advisor on the school paper I wrote for and I liked her class, too, because she read books to us such as *Treasure Island* and *Great Expectations*. Some kids just slept through the hour while she read, but I always listened, she told a story so well.

Another I liked best was my French teacher, Olive Mazurek, even though she gave us more homework than any other teacher and gave the toughest tests. She was good because she made everyone work and try to do their best, and we respected her because we couldn't pull anything over on her like we could most of the other teachers.

It was easy to snow our social studies teacher, "Peroxide Powers." She was a bleached blonde who always wore sunglasses to class on Monday mornings, nursing a hangover from the weekend. She seldom taught us anything on Mondays but would tell the class to read our text book for the hour. All except three girls in the front row who buttered up to her. She would send one of them out to the neighborhood grocery store for some black coffee and aspirin, then put the other two to work combing her hair and polishing her nails.

It was I, incidentally, who gave Miss Powers her nickname. I gave most of my teachers and classmates nicknames, sometimes referring to how they looked or acted, or just tagged them with names from characters in movies I'd see. "Hot Lips," "Tampico," and "Breathless" were names I gave to some of the girls in my classes. It was pretty racy for a boy who had only seen one pair of girls' panties, and that by accident.

I began to acquire a reputation for having a sense of humor, albeit an odd one. It came out of me sometimes without warning, like a zit.

One day it came out at Al Barradell, our algebra teacher. He also was as round as he was tall, but was taller than Dorothy Bailey. He too always wore sunglasses in class, but didn't seem to have hangovers. It was just his way, perhaps to try to hide from us behind his tinted lenses.

One day Mister Barradell studied a problem in our algebra book, of course through his sunglasses, and then asked the class,

"Why can't I understand this problem?"

No one replied and a long silence followed. I couldn't hold myself back, so I ventured an explanation: "Because you can't see it. You're wearing dark glasses."

Mr. Barradell sent me out of the room for the rest of the period for that smart remark, but I thought it had been worth it.

I didn't have to be funny with our biology teacher. She did the job herself. Johanna Fielding walked like Groucho Marx, bent over almost horizontally at the waist and with her caboose trailing far behind the rest of her. No beauty to begin with, her posture and walk gave her an odd appearance, but she was a good science teacher. She gave a lecture to us freshmen one day that was close to telling about the birds and bees, only she did it with frogs. It still wasn't all that clear to most of us in the class.

My home room teacher, Mrs. Barron, was very nice, but after our freshman year she died. Her replacement was a new art and drama teacher, George Dunn, and we liked him as much or even more. It was he who got me into acting in school plays.

First I played a father in a one-act domestic comedy, using flour to whiten my dark brown hair. Mr. Dunn thought I could handle a full-length play after that and cast me as Randolph, the tall, lanky kid-brother to the heroine in "A Date With Judy." I looked at the playbook and got scared because Randolph had dialogue on almost every page of the three-act play and was on-stage almost every minute of it.

Somehow I memorized the part and knew I was physically right for it. If I could only remember my lines and get the laughs my dialogue ought to generate.

When the curtain went up on the first act, I was to be alone on the stage, sitting on a couch and trying to fix an alarm clock. I was to speak what I was thinking, but as the curtain raised, I forgot my opening lines.

I strained my ears to hear one of the three prompters who were trying to feed my lines to me from either side of the stage and from the orchestra pit, but couldn't hear them. I thought everyone in the audience of the darkened theater knew I'd forgotten my lines and was going to boo me off the stage, but still couldn't hear any of the prompters.

To stall until I might remember my lines, I tugged and prodded at the clock and managed to get some laughs that hadn't been in the script. After what seemed like hours but was only seconds, I remembered my lines and didn't forget any of them during the rest of the play.

Every funny line I spoke during the three acts drew more laughs than I expected. After the play I realized something I'd never known before. I was funny.

The curtain calls were further proof that I had done a good job. The rest of the cast of the play asked me to join them at a party afterward. I wanted to go, but couldn't. I had been so nervous during the play, I peed in my pants!

The next day at school, I realized something new. I was popular. Classmates I'd never even seen before congratulated me in the halls and I felt something else. I was liked. It felt good to be liked.

Not that it did me any good with the girls. They seemed to think of me as a brother but not as date material, although I really didn't know anyone in my four years of high school who was really dating, much less "going steady". It wasn't easy to date because for one thing, no one had a car. If any guy took a girl to a movie, they both walked.

The only guy I knew who dated girls was the heavy smoker, Kasimir, and that figured because he was tall and dark-haired and the best-looking guy in school.

One Friday in autumn it got around school that Kaz was going to "go all the way" with a girl that night. Some of us had to check that out!

After school, Bonehead and Ostrowski and I went to Kaz's house and waited until he left it. Then we followed from a distance as he went to the drug store. Looking inside the window, we saw him asking the pharmacist for something at the prescription counter. The man frowned, then smiled, and gave Kaz a small package. Kaz immediately put it in his pants pocket. I figured it was one of those things you're supposed to put on if you go messing around with a girl.

We hid behind a car when Kaz left the drug store and followed him again. He went to a garage a few blocks away that had been closed for about a year, and waited. My pals and I waited too, from behind a truck parked nearby.

While Kaz waited, he began to shiver. It wasn't that cold out, and I wondered if he was just nervous.

After about ten long minutes, a car pulled up and a girl got out. I'd never seen her before and figured she wasn't from our high school, but she was pretty and wore bluejeans and a sweater, just like Kaz. Kaz took her around back of the garage and we saw them enter through a door he'd somehow managed to get open.

Once they were inside, Bonehead and Ostrowski and I ran behind the garage where there was a shed and some old tires stacked. There was an empty orange crate beneath one of the small windows and I got up on it.

I saw Kaz turn on a naked light bulb and my heart began to pound. I was going to see the school's biggest, and probably only, makeout artist at work!

"What's going on inside?" Bonehead asked eagerly.

"Let me see!" Ostrowski demanded.

"There ain't room up here for two," I said. "Wait until something happens, then I'll tell you guys about it."

The garage looked dirty and dumpy inside. An old car stood rusting alongside some oil drums.

An old couch stood against one wall. It was a faded red color, with dumb flowers printed all over it. Kaz took the girl by an arm and walked her up to it. They stood in front of the couch and looked at each other. Kaz pushed some dusty magazines and newspapers off of it and onto the floor.

After clearing off the couch, Kaz just sort of stood there. The girl quick kissed him on the mouth and he looked as if he didn't know how to kiss her back.

"She's French-kissing him!" I reported to the guys.

I had never put my tongue inside a girl's mouth and wondered if I'd like it. I didn't think I would. But then, I had never kissed a girl on the lips or anywhere else, so what did I know?

"The girl's shaking her head at Kaz," I told my pals. "She doesn't seem to think much of his kissing."

"What are they doing now?" Bonehead and Ostrowski asked in unison.

I began giving them an ongoing report, sounding like a radio announcer at a Joe Louis fight:

"She's starting to take off her sweater. Kaz's starting to take his off. She's reaching out and hugging him. He's letting her, but doesn't hug her back. She's looking at him moony-eyed and kissing him again."

Bonehead and Ostrowski were just about going crazy, wanting to get on the box with me and see for themselves and I almost fell off.

I wished I could hear what they were saying but couldn't hear anything from inside the garage.

"What's happening now?" the guys both asked.

181

"Aw, let's go," I said.

"Go?" Bonehead asked. "Now?"

I had to hold Ostrowski by an arm to keep him from taking my place on top the box.

"We've seen enough," I said.

"We haven't seen anything!" Bonehead and Ostrowski said in unison again.

I felt sort of guilty, watching Kaz and his girl. Maybe it was because I got the feeling he'd never done whatever he was doing before. Besides, I didn't think I was going to learn much from Kaz anyway. He sure wasn't the Errol Flynn he made everyone think he was.

As my pals and I walked away from the garage, I wondered if Kaz was having a good time. I hoped he was, as I hoped I would, when my turn would come.

Chapter Sixteen

Praise the Lord, and pass the ammunition!

As the war went on, we were lucky. Johnny and none of the uncles or cousins in the family had been injured or killed.

My sister probably came the closest of all of us at home to real danger those years. She had a bad toothache and had to go to the dentist, but most dentists had been drafted into the service. Old dentists came out of retirement to take their place and Sis had to go to one of them.

I went along and cringed as Mary sat in the dentist's chair and he started to work in her mouth. It was because he had such old equipment. I wouldn't have wanted him to work on my sore tooth with a drill so old it wasn't even electric. It was wood. He got it going by a foot pedal!

We on the home front knew it, too. War *was* hell!

In his letters home to me from duty on ship in the Pacific, my brother kept hounding me to leave my job at the candy store and find "real" work somewhere else. Finally, I followed his advice. While in my sophomore year in high school, I went to work in the shipping department at Wieboldt's department store a few miles away on Milwaukee Avenue.

My job, along with a half-dozen other teenage boys and older men was to wrap purchases customers had made which were to be delivered to their homes by mail or truck. I learned how to wrap delicate dishes and lamps so they wouldn't break in transit, and how to secure a box with string or rope so it would stay tied. I worked after school on Monday and Thursday nights until the store closed at 10 p.m., and all day on Saturdays.

I met someone on that job who was everything I wished I was or could be. Freddie Hartzell, a curly-brown-haired, good-looking All-American boy, became my first real best friend at work or school or anywhere. He was always cheerful and pretending to be playing basketball, dribbling an invisible ball along the floor or leaping up and shooting it into an imaginary hoop.

Freddie and I and some other older guys spent the day packing up the merchandise to be shipped. Then he and I and another guy a little older than us named Melvin loaded everything into a big truck that was parked outside in the back of the store.

One night, while I was inside loading the truck, Freddie and Mel were tossing packages to me and I stacked them far up front so they wouldn't fall. I heard Mel whispering something to Freddie and wondered what they were talking about.

Mel suddenly slammed the doors on the back of the truck together. Then he slid the bolt across and closed the padlock.

Now I knew what they had been whispering about. Mel decided to play a prank on me, locking me inside the truck.

It was pitch black inside the truck and I was a little scared, but figured they wouldn't keep me locked up in there for long. I lost track of time until finally I heard Freddie ask Mel to open the doors and let me out. Those were about the longest minutes I ever lived, and I was glad when Freddie finally let me out.

They had been only horsing around, but I had the feeling Mel didn't like me because Freddie and I had become such good friends. I wished Freddie hadn't gone along with the prank. I'd never have done it to him.

Besides the pay, working in the department store had its special benefits. Rationing was still on, and toilet paper was often out of stock in the grocery stores. Special sales were held for Wieboldt's employees when shipments of such scarce commodities came in. I got in line with the other employees and was able to buy and bring home a half dozen or dozen "piano rolls." On rare occasions, I also bought nylon stockings for Mom when they were impossible to find in other stores.

My sister and I were together a lot during our high school years when our brother was away in the war. We went to the movies every chance we got. One day we saw a rerun of "The Wizard of Oz" and when Judy Garland was about to sing "Over the Rainbow," a drunk sitting in front of us said, very sadly, "Sing it, Judy!" I wondered what his sad story was.

We went to the movies not only to escape into another world but because we liked the actors and actresses. Errol Flynn, Gary Cooper, and Ronald Colman became my heroes and role models because I didn't see any around like them in my life. Irene Dunne and Barbara Stanwyck were like second mothers to me. For aunts and uncles, there were character actors such as Fay Bainter and Una O'Connor, Walter Huston and Frank Morgan, and dozens of others we saw three or four times a year in their new movies. We saw them as often as we saw our own aunts and uncles; maybe even more often.

Mary and I began writing fan letters to our favorite actors and actresses and got autographed portraits in return, sometimes even letters from them.

The relative we saw the most of was our bachelor Aunt Mary, my mother's eldest sister, because she came around often. She worked on the assembly line at Western Electric in Cicero and had an apartment on Chicago's North Side.

She was a thin, sweet woman with a soft voice that could put you to sleep. She read most of the L. Frank Baum Oz books to us kids, introducing us to more than just the Wizard of Oz but to the Gnome King, Glinda the Good, and other characters in a fantasy world of a dozen books many years before Harry Potter took over that genre of fiction for kids.

Baum, by the way, had been a Chicago newspaper reporter when he wrote the first Oz book that took the literary world by storm and kept adding new books to the series for decades.

When we were teenagers, Sis Mary and I took a streetcar ride to Aunt Mary's apartment a few miles away on Armitage Avenue near Halsted Street. By then she had married and she and her husband had a small one-bedroom apartment on the second floor behind Nick Stitch's Funeral Home.

It was always scary to go through the alley to the stairway to Aunt Mary's flat because we passed the back of the undertaking parlor where caskets were kept and bodies were prepared for wakes.

Aunt Mary's husband, also named Walter, was very nice to me and my sister and brother, but wasn't well. Soon after they married, he was diagnosed with tuberculosis. He spent several years in a sanitarium before dying.

I remember him best for having a phonograph turntable that could cut blank 12-inch records. I watched, as a fascinated teenager, while he cut me one of Rimsky-Korsakov's Antar Symphony. I played it often at home on a small phonograph that was in a box like a suitcase. Uncle Walter would have loved the technology that came years later for recording music.

Several years after Aunt Mary's husband died, she remarried. The night before the wedding was hot and she put an electric fan on the floor by her bed. When she got up during the night, she forgot the fan was there and stubbed her toe on it. It hurt so much she had to have it bandaged. The next morning at her wedding, Aunt Mary walked up the center aisle at the church with a limp. She wore one high-heeled dress shoe on her good foot and a house slipper on her sore one.

Sometimes Mom and Dad took Sis and me along when they visited their old friends, Buck and Edna. First they owned a small restaurant and some Sunday afternoons we helped them by washing dishes. After their restaurant failed, they opened a dry cleaners, but they went broke on that, too.

Edna died soon after that and Buck got a job as doorman at a hotel on the Near North Side at Division Street near Broadway. Sometimes I rode a streetcar there after school and visited with him for an hour. Then after a few more years, he passed on too. We missed them because they were two of our oldest friends.

My sister hadn't gotten an after-school job because our mother asked her to help at home, housekeeping and preparing meals while Mom worked. Mary did this until she turned sixteen the following March, 1945. Then she went to work part-time as an operator at the telephone company, but in a different office than the one Mom worked in. Sis was a junior at Wells High School while I was a sophomore and she worked two days a week after school from 4 to 10 p.m. and all-day Saturdays or Sundays.

Sis worked eighteen hours a week and earned a dollar an hour. Eighteen dollars a week was big money to her. To help out at home, she gave Mom $5 a week for her room and board and began paying for her own school books, clothes, and her life insurance premium.

The telephone exchange Mary worked at required her to take two trolley lines. She had to change trolleys and wait for the next one at an intersection just west of downtown Chicago which was a rather seedy part of the city. The trolley stop was in front of a striptease establishment called "The Star and Garter." On rainy or cold days, Sis stood in the enclosed front doorway for shelter, trying not to be noticed by the men who came to see the show inside.

With just an hour between the end of the school day at 3 o'clock and having to be on the job at 4 p.m., there was never time for an early dinner, so Sis usually wolfed down some milk and cookies or a piece of pie. If she had homework the next day and had to work after school, she would do it on the trolleys to and from the telephone switchboard. It wasn't easy, but she often did her shorthand homework on the swerving, rocking trolleys.

By the time she got back home at about eleven o'clock at night, she was too tired to eat and just went to bed. It wasn't easy, but she liked the work and, even more, the pay and the sense of independence the job gave her.

In April, 1945, a month after Mary became a telephone operator, F.D.R. died. That May, Hitler was dead and Germany surrendered.

Both Mom and Sis were at their switchboards on V-E (Victory in Europe) Day, May 7, 1945.

"I still get goose pimples remembering," Sis told me years later. "So many people were calling their loved ones about the great news, the switchboards lit up like Christmas trees. Callers were laughing and crying and it was wonderful."

On August 6, an atomic bomb was dropped on Hiroshima and the Japanese surrendered soon after. Mom and Mary were on duty again on V-J (Victory in Japan) Day, August 14, when the war with Japan ended.

After serving out his four-year enlistment in the Navy, my brother returned home in 1947. Mom had a special treat waiting for him. She baked his favorite, a three-layer banana cake with white frosting. We all sat down at the kitchen table and watched as he ate about half of it and drank a whole quart of milk.

Johnny showed us a Japanese sword he brought back as a souvenir. He had presents, too. A porcelain geisha-girl doll in ornate costume for Sis, though she'd outgrown dolls by then, and authentic Japanese silk kimonos for Mom and Dad. He gave me a small Japanese flag showing the rising sun and some Japanese candy.

I was glad my brother was back home, especially after he told me how deep my voice had gotten while he was away.

He only told me about the money he'd won shooting craps aboard ship and in Tokyo, because he didn't want Mom to know he gambled. When a dice game got really going, if his shipmates didn't have any more money to toss down, they gambled their souvenirs or personal belongings.

Taking one pot, Johnny not only won a couple of hundred dollars, but a custom-made blue silk sailor suit. A shipmate who had no more money to bet had put up the suit of Navy blues a Japanese tailor in Tokyo had made for him. Johnny didn't bring it home with him. He lost it later in another crap game.

I wondered if my brother had the gambling bug in him, as our father had. I hoped he hadn't. I didn't think I had inherited it and was glad.

Johnny told us that his most exciting war adventure happened one night at sea. A bad storm had built up and he had "the watch," the Navy's term for guard duty. He had to walk guard on top the deck in the storm while everyone else was below sleeping or resting.

The storm made the small ship toss in the high wind. Huge waves washed over the deck, making it slippery. After one big wave crashed over, Johnny felt himself sliding to one side of the ship. It was too dark to see where a guard rail was, but as he slid toward where he thought it was, he tried reaching out and grabbing hold of it. But he kept sliding and thought he must have slid past the railing. In another moment, he expected to be washed overboard.

Just when he thought he was going to slide off the deck and into the ocean, a hand reached out from behind. It held him by the left shoulder. Johnny felt himself being pulled back until he found the railing and held it tight. When he looked around, he didn't see anyone. He then walked the entire deck, but didn't see anyone there.

After his watch was up, Johnny went down below in the ship and asked who had come up to rescue him from being washed overboard. To a man, his shipmates said they hadn't gone topside while he was on his watch.

Then, Johnny wondered, whose hand had saved him from drowning?

There is no logical explanation to my brother's mysterious experience at sea. Those who believe in ghosts could accept that perhaps there are spirits of sailors who drowned at sea who look after and protect their living comrades. Movies have been made on this theme, as was suggested of pilots in the Spencer Tracy World War II classic, "A Guy Named Joe," which was recently remade about firefighting pilots with Richard Dreyfuss in "Always."

Johnny had always been prone to telling ghost stories when we were boys, but I tended to believe him this time.

There was another strange war story I learned a few years after the war, on another visit at Grandpa's house on Peoria Street, after my uncles had returned uninjured. Aunt Edith, another of my father's cousins, told us what had happened to her son, whose name also was Johnny.

My cousin Johnny was a tall, strapping young man who had joined the Navy. His mother wanted to make sure he had a good weapon on him, not trusting the government to issue him one. She bought him a hunting knife and had his name carved on it.

Johnny took the knife with him to war in the Pacific. One day when his ship was hit, he found himself floating in the ocean with some of his shipmates. A school of sharks came swimming toward them. Johnny was the only one with a weapon on him, since he always carried the knife his mother had given him. Swimming away from his mates, he swam out and wrestled with the lead shark, slitting its belly open with the knife. The blood that spilled out attracted the other sharks and they fed on the one Johnny killed. Before the sharks finished their meal and could attack the sailors holding onto life preservers in the water, a ship came by and rescued them all.

In wrestling with the shark, Johnny's tailbone got cut by the shark and became infected. He spent the rest of his life in a naval hospital. After he was there a couple of years, he got a package in the mail. It was from a ship captain he'd never heard of before, so he opened the package wondering what was in it.

Johnny found his knife inside the package. He had left it in the shark when he cut it open. The captain wrote that a sailor on watch on his ship had spotted something shiny floating on the surface of the ocean. When they brought the ship up alongside, they discovered it was a knife that was stuck in a shark's bone. Johnny's name was on it and the captain found out where to send it.

I wish Cousin Johnny's story could have ended happier but after years in the naval hospital, he died. His mother kept the knife until years later when she passed on.

The war changed a lot of lives, during and after. Nothing was quite the same anymore, even on the home front. It could be seen in many ways both big and small.

After the war, many people traded their old ice boxes in for new electric refrigerators. So did we and it was wonderful not to have to empty the ice pan anymore. We had to always empty the pan under the ice box before we went anywhere, especially to the movies, and again the minute we got back. If the pan wasn't emptied for the four hours it took to see most double features, water would overflow and spill onto the kitchen floor and have to be mopped up. A refrigerator was a convenience and a luxury we never thought we would have in our kitchen.

My mother and sister stunk up the whole house every Friday night setting their hair. They used an awful-smelling goo that came in new do-it-yourself permanent wave kits.

A new daily morning newspaper was starting in Chicago and there was a contest to give it a name. My father thought up two good ones to enter: *The Chicago Sun* and *The Windy City Sun*. As luck had it, he chose the latter name to enter and lost. The name selected was *The Chicago Sun*. That was about as close as he came to winning anything. He seemed to have luck like that.

So many babies were being born when the servicemen came home after the war that my father thought a new kind of diaper would be useful. He came up with the idea of making disposable diapers. Unfortunately, Dad didn't do anything with the idea. Someone else did and became a millionaire.

My brother didn't stay home long, after he returned from the Navy. Mary graduated from high school and at her first class reunion she introduced Johnny to her former locker partner, a very pretty girl. He began dating her and soon they married.

It was a big Polish wedding and the reception was held at a Catholic church hall with a polka band. All the relatives came and danced, drank, and ate tons of food which wasn't catered but prepared by all the ladies in both families.

During the wedding supper, the priest who had married Johnny and his bride began passing a plate from table to table. Guests were asked to put money onto it. Johnny got up and took the priest aside, saying a collection was embarrassing and anyway, he'd paid for the service. The priest smiled and explained, "The money isn't for the church. It's for the groom, to help cover expenses of the wedding."

Johnny told the priest, "Carry on, Father!"

At Polish weddings, everyone gets to dance with the bride, but it cost $5 per dance. Another custom has the bride taking off her wedding garter and auctioning it. All the money helps the couple get a new start in life.

A lot of people who survived the war were getting new starts in life. For others, it was pretty much business as usual. My mother and father were still fighting their economic war.

I was still wondering how frogs did it.

Chapter Seventeen

To each his own, to each his own,
and my own is you

Four years of high school go too fast. At the end, all a person remembers is class bells ringing and a few highlights of friendships and good and bad times.

I learned about Colonial history, how to multiply to the tenth power, take a flower apart and study a pistol and stamen, could find Mozambique on a map of Africa, and sometimes knew a pronoun from a past participle, but still knew next to nothing about girls.

Dance class didn't help. Every Friday afternoon the boys lined up on one side of the gym and the girls on the other and we tried to learn "social dancing." That meant boys and girls danced a waltz or two-step (a "box waltz") without hardly touching.

Two gym teachers always chaperoned the dance classes, a man and a woman. They taught us boys to bow to the girls and ask for a dance, then it was a slow twirl on the gym floor to some scratchy record, and you couldn't hold the girl close. A waltzing elephant could have fit between the boys and their dance partners.

It didn't really matter because I never fell for any of the girls at school and didn't even have the "hots" for any of them. Maybe that was because I was so loyal to Jane Powell and also the Virgin Mary.

I joked a lot with the girls and worked with them in plays and on the school newspaper, but didn't have a crush on any of them.

One tall, pretty, dark-haired girl named Florence, kind of a "hot number" in one of my classes, turned to ask me something one afternoon. Her boyfriend, a tough-looking senior, was looking through the window in the hall just then and got the idea I was trying to put the make on his girl. I became pretty scared that he was going to grab me after class and kill me or something.

But I guess Florence explained to him that I wasn't flirting with her, I was just giving her the answer to a test question, because he left me alone. Afterward, I kind of wished she hadn't explained it to him the way she did, as if I sure wouldn't be anyone for him to be jealous about. It made me feel kind of like a loser with girls. I didn't like that feeling much, even though I thought I probably *was* a loser with girls.

If I was shy with girls, I did have some guts when it came to standing up for my principles. Here's how that came about.

The most popular thing in the monthly school paper was a column which poked fun at both students and teachers and satirized just about everything. Two of the best writers on the paper wrote the column and got their own bylines, but the column was called "Orville and Ditsy." As the writers who wrote under those names graduated, new writers replaced them. The column was one of the longest-running features of the paper and had been going for decades.

After I had been on the paper about a year and was a junior, writing news and features, a graduating senior who was the "Ditsy" half of the "Orville and Ditsy" team asked if I would like to replace him for my junior and senior year. Only winning an Academy Award for best screenplay or the Pulitzer Prize for best novel would have been a higher honor and I accepted joyfully.

I wrote as Ditsy very well with a senior named Irving Hilgebrand who was the Orville half of the team. The column continued to be the most read thing in the paper, until halfway through the school year when a new English teacher was assigned to be the faculty advisor to the school paper, replacing Dorothy Bailey.

The new advisor, a tall, starchy type by the name of Mrs. McGruder, called me into her office one day and laid this bomb on me:

"From now on, I want the Orville and Ditsy column to just report on the Student Council meetings."

I couldn't believe it. "No laughs, no poking fun at anyone?"

"Student Council meetings," Mrs. McGruder said.

"Have you told Irving?" I asked.

She replied with confidence. "He says that's okay with him, if it has to be."

I didn't even have to think about it.

"I'd rather see the column die," I told her.

She looked me coldly in the eyes. "Then it will die," she said, and it did.

It had been my greatest achievement in high school, being co-author of that humor column. I gained a certain amount of status from it, but was surprised to discover how much greater admiration the other students had for me, after I stood up to Mrs. McGruder and let the column die rather than let her sanitize it.

It also was my first lesson in Freedom of Speech under the First Amendment to the Constitution and I believed I passed the test.

I stayed on the paper and wrote news and features after that, but it was never the same. The fun had gone out of it.

I began spending more time in school plays, and felt I had a mentor in my home room teacher, Mister Dunn. He was the most encouraging teacher I ever had, and the nicest. I even forgave him for casting me as "The Voice of Truth" in the school Christmas pageant that winter.

My role was the biggest and longest in the pageant, but I wouldn't be on-stage a minute of it. I was to be up in a heating ventilator high up and to one side of the stage, behind a grill, speaking as if I was the Lord Himself. I was like the narrator in a Shakespeare play or the Chorus in a Greek tragedy, reading lines that sounded as if they were written for a gospel by one of the saints.

My delivery in rehearsals disturbed Mister Dunn. "Wally, you have to say your lines in a deeper voice and with more authority," he advised me. "Do you go to church?"

I said yes, every Sunday.

"Then next Sunday, listen to how the priest gives his sermon. Read your lines that way."

I listened at church the next Sunday when the priest gave his sermon, which was a novelty for me because my mind usually drifted during that part of the Mass. I caught what Mister Dunn had in mind.

At the next rehearsal, I read my lines like Moses pronouncing on the Mount. Charlton Heston would have been proud of me.

"That's it!" Mister Dunn beamed. "You've got it!"

I had it, and most people liked it at the opening performance a few weeks later, except a little boy who sat in his mother's lap in the middle of the school auditorium. Every time I opened my mouth and read a line, as Moses like as I could, the boy began howling and wailing. I was scaring the diapers off of him!

Nonetheless, I continued in my best Moses voice and afterward Mister Dunn said the whole cast, me included, had done fine. And I hadn't peed in my pants.

Two other things happened about then that related to religion in my life. One was, my mother advised my sister and me, "Go to Mass every Sunday and be a good Catholic, but don't be 'churchy.'"

I think she said that because of the part in the Bible when Jesus accuses the Pharisees of praying a good religion but not really practicing it. Following Mom's advice, I grew up to become what I call a "closet Catholic," going to Mass every Sunday, putting my donation in the collection basket, and doing my best to obey the Ten Commandments, but not joining any clubs. Charlton Heston, Mother knows best.

I also still wish the Mass was in Latin. Like opera is better when you hear it in Italian which you don't quite understand. I think it all has to do with sustaining the mystery.

The other thing that touched on religion about then in my young life was what happened one night when I learned what happens physically to a boy when he becomes sexually excited. I didn't know what it was called, but knew by how good it felt that it had to be a sin, so I confessed it to old Father Kaminsky that following Saturday at St. Stanislaus Church.

Sure enough, the number of Hail Mary's the priest gave me was enough to convince me it was one of the most mortal of sins.

But I still didn't know what it was, or was called, and I didn't know anyone I could ask about it. So I went to the library and looked for a book that might give me some clue. After a long search of medical and health books and not finding anything that sounded like what I was looking for, I found a book called *Boys and Sex*. With a title like that, how could I miss?

The only thing was, the book looked like it was about fifty years old. No one had checked it out on their library card since about 1908. I wouldn't either. The librarian was an old lady and my face would be red as a tomato if she looked at the title, so I read the book there.

In one chapter on good and bad health practices, the author mentioned something that I thought had to be what happened to me more about then and that I always had to confess. He said it was one of the worst things you could do, because if you did it often enough, you could go blind or crazy.

Now I knew what it was that made me feel so good but at the same time so guilty. But I still never mentioned the M word to my father or brother or any of my pals, and wondered if they were going blind or crazy, too.

One of the things the author advised boys in order to "control the sex urge" was to keep themselves busy. It was about the same as what Father Kaminsky kept telling me in the confessional,

"Idle hands and minds are the devil's tools. Avoid the occasion of sin by keeping your mind and body pure. One of the best ways of doing this is to keep busy so your thoughts don't stray onto temptation."

My father had never talked to me about "the birds and the bees." The only thing he ever told me on that subject was, "If you can't handle it, keep it in your pants."

That made me understand later why he always had Johnny Boy and me sleep with our hands on top of the blanket.

I thought I was already busy enough with studies and my after-school job in the department store, but took the advice and became even busier. I took on a nonpaying job at school. It had been kind of a slave labor plan by our principal, Paul Revere Polk. Maybe he thought it up with the help of the building superintendent, a fancy word for janitor, whose name was Jesse James Boone. Together they were a regular American history book.

Paul Revere's plan was that each student had to do some volunteer work each semester for one of the teachers. Our political science teacher, Mister Gorman, a tall, thin man whose face matched his gray hair and who always looked as if he was sucking on a lemon, was in need of an office helper. He interviewed me.

"Have you taken mechanical drawing?" he asked, sizing me up suspiciously as not being up to the tasks he had in mind for his helper.

I was glad he asked that, because I had taken a course in mechanical drawing. In fact, my industrial arts teacher had given me a B-plus for preparing painstakingly-drawn India ink three-dimensional diagrams of buildings and objects.

"Yes, sir, I have taken mechanical drawing," I replied. I'd love to do some technical drawing for him and wondered what project he had in mind for me that involved mechanical drawing skills.

"Good," Mister Gorman said, then handed me a sheet of typing paper and a ruler. "If you have a pencil, would you draw some vertical lines on this?"

I worked dutifully one hour a week for Mister Gorman but, after that initial encounter, couldn't stand the man.

Later my volunteer work took me up to a room on the fourth floor of the school where text books were stored. Two other students and I had absolutely nothing to do there, so we tore pages out of some of the books and shaped them into airplanes and little helicopters and sailed them out of the windows. We watched as they flew or floated down onto the busy intersection below. That was about as mischievous as I ever got in school.

By my senior year I was both busy and popular and was accepted by both the student leaders of the school -- of which I was one, but hardly realized it -- and by the rougher guys who just sat around and smoked and got excited every time a skirt walked by.

We had a substitute math teacher that year who drove the rougher guys wild. She sat on the front of her desk and dangled her legs. The guys, who normally sat in the back of the room, fought each other for the front-row seats.

A little covey of the six smartest girls in the class always had the front-row seats with the regular math teacher and had gotten most of her time and attention. In the sub's class, they had to take seats behind the drooling boys and were pretty much ignored.

Occasionally, I was still wising-off to teachers. My French teacher, Olive Mazurek, who was tall, lean, and businesslike, had taken the first half of my senior year off to study in Paris. She returned for the final semester of our French class. A substitute who had taken her place had been so easy to snow, we hadn't gotten much work done in Miss Mazurek's absence.

"What book are you on?" Miss Mazurek asked the class on her first day back in command.

A long silence followed as no one in the room dared reply.

"Same book," I volunteered from my desk in about the middle of the room.

Miss Mazurek looked distressed. "What chapter?" she asked.

Again, a long silence from the class.

"Same chapter," I said.

The rest of the class sat frozen as Miss Mazurek stoically absorbed that bit of information, then asked the most dangerous question of all:

"What page are you on?"

After the usual silence, I responded,

"Same page."

None of my classmates dared to laugh, until they saw the slight grin on Miss Mazurek's face.

"All right then, class," she said. "We have work to do."

I didn't know it at the time, but I had made a friend in Miss Mazurek. She appeared to be made of ice, but I got the feeling I had melted her a little with my bit of humor.

I worked my butt off for her and got B's because I deserved them. I figured she liked me enough to give me A's, but we respected each other too much for that.

Two years after graduating, I returned to Wells for my transfer of credits to go to college and Miss Mazurek was the only teacher I cared to visit. When she saw me looking in the window of her room, she told her class to read their texts and invited me to come in and sit beside her desk. We had a long talk, about the "good old days."

My brother had been right about working away from home. I liked the job, the store, the friends I made there, and the money I earned. When summer vacation came, I worked full-time and liked the extra money. I gave some to Mom to help out, and she let me keep some for spending money.

Every Friday after we got our pay, my friend Freddie Hartzell and I went up to the music department and bought records. A real nice girl there increased my interest in classical music. Back in the early 1940s phonograph records were thick and heavy, ten or twelve inches in diameter. Each payday the clerk recommended I buy one classical record or album, a recording of the overture to an opera or something else with a lot of melody such as "The Anvil Chorus" or "The 1812 Overture."

I got to like the classical records, but still not as much as the songs on the Hit Parade in 1947 and 1948. I bought a record of just about every popular song that came out, like "Chi-Baba Chi-Baba," "Open the Door, Richard," "Woody Woodpecker," "I've Got a Lovely Bunch of Coconuts," and Doris Day singing "It's Magic." I never had the courage to buy and bring home a record of "Careless Hands."

My mother and father were still arguing a lot because he was not any more dependable about coming home with his pay. To try to make up for what he lost in gambling, Dad started working two jobs. By then he was a motorman driving the elevated trains in Chicago and began moonlighting some evenings and weekends at the big amusement park, Riverview. My sister and I took the streetcar out there and watched Dad strapping people into their seats to go up on the parachute ride.

We went on the Bobbs and the other roller coasters, but never got the courage to go on the parachutes. People sat in seats like park swings and were lifted high above the amusement park so they could see all over the city. Without knowing when, as they reached the top of the ride, the parachute opened above them and they glided between some rails back down to the ground.

Our favorite thing at Riverview was going through Aladdin's Castle. It was a big spook house where every dark room we entered had something scary, such as a gorilla's hairy arm reaching out to grab us.

One summer vacation when I was laid off at Wieboldt's I went to work at Riverview myself. My job was to run the KiddieLand rides -- a small Ferris wheel, tilt-a-whirl, merry-go-round, and train. One afternoon some little boy stood up in the train and fell out. I raced to the main switch and stopped the train just before it could roll over him. I wondered why the park people hadn't put Dad on the KiddieLand job and me on the parachute job. His looked a lot easier. But that made sense and I learned early that a lot of jobs or bosses don't.

That fall I got hired again at Wieboldt's but Freddie didn't come back to work. I never saw him again. It wasn't as much fun working in the shipping room anymore. The other guys weren't anywhere near as nice as Freddie had been, and work became more like a job. In it's own little way, it taught me to try and like what you work at, because you can't depend on people you work with to make the job satisfying.

After school one day in my senior year, Bonehead came knocking at our door. "A ghost's throwing things around in our house!" he cried.

Ghosts again!, I thought. I don't know what help he thought I would be, but he asked me to go home with him and see the ghost for myself.

He lived with his mother in the rear apartment of a two-story building across the street. When we got there, I saw a mess. Chairs were overturned in the kitchen, dishes lay broken on the floor, a lamp had fallen from a table in the living room, and pictures on the walls hung topsy-turvy.

His mother, a thin old woman, was distraught and sobbing in the kitchen, looking even more pale than usual. "Go get Father Kaminsky!" she cried.

Bonehead and I ran four blocks to St. Stanislaus Church and interrupted the overweight pastor during his meditation. When the priest heard that ghosts were haunting Bonehead's house, he grabbed a little black satchel and followed us on-the-run.

"This is the third time," Bonehead's mother explained to the priest when we returned with him. "A man died in this flat once. His ghost must haunt the place."

"It may be a poltergeist," Father Kaminsky said. "Sometimes if a person dies violently, their spirit comes back to make mischief."

He took no chances. Father Kaminsky took a crucifix out of his case and blessed the apartment. Then he went from room to room, sloshing holy water on everything and chanting in Latin. It must have worked because after that, Bonehead never complained again about things flying around at home.

Helping Bonehead with his ghost kept me busy, too, but I still had something to confess every Saturday, still didn't have a girlfriend, and still knew from nothing about sex.

The problem, I decided, was no girl really turned me on. Except Jane Powell and she was in Hollywood and too far away to date. What I needed was a pretty girl who lived within walking distance who would like a nice quiet guy who liked to go to the movies and write stories but who wasn't Errol Flynn. At least not yet.

What I did start to get to feel was, somewhere out there was the girl for me. I just had to wait for her to come along or work harder to find her. There was somebody for everybody. To each his own, as the song hit of 1946 promised.

I thought if I liked someone as much as my cousin Betty from Anderson did, I'd find the right girl for me. Betty used to come to Chicago every few weekends to see someone she must have liked very much. He lived at the Lincoln Park Zoo. Chicago's big, famous, hairy gorilla, Bushman.

To each his own.

Before I knew it, I was close to graduation from high school and still didn't know much about girls. Take for example the party some of our class put together at one of the guys' houses. We played "spin the bottle" and I thought it was a pretty dumb way for two people to get to kiss. But when Eleanor Eulenberg whom I didn't go for at all kissed me, I thought I kind of liked the game. With my eyes closed, she could have been Jane Powell.

Then I showed how dumb I was. In another party game, Eleanor put her arm around my shoulder and asked,

"What's the first thing you'd take off, if you were going to undress and go to bed?"

The rules were, you had to actually take off whatever you said you would before going to bed.

Heck, I didn't know.

"My shoes," I said.

Everyone laughed their sides out and, as I took off my shoes, Eleanor told me, "What next?"

"My socks," I said.

That got even more laughs as I took them off.

"What next?" she prompted.

I had to think hard. What else could I take off that wouldn't be too embarrassing?

"My sweater," I said.

I had everyone practically rolling on the floor as I took off my sweater. Eleanor kept her arm around my shoulder and asked me the same question as before.

I was not in any hurry to take off my shirt, which I figured would be next, when I saw Bonehead giving me a hint and realized the joke was on me. I took Eleanor's arm from around my shoulder and felt as if I hadn't learned a single thing about girls.

I never had much fun in gym class in school. I still never caught on about what to do with a basketball or football if I caught one. I hated swimming most of all because for the final exam, everyone was supposed to dive off the diving board. I swam like a rock and had absolutely no idea how to coordinate breathing with my arms and legs in the water.

Just before the final exam in swimming, some mystic predicted the world was going to come to an end, at noon the next day. It was in the newspaper and on the radio and I thought, swell! My swim class was going to meet at one o'clock the next day. If the world did come to an end at noon, I wouldn't have to dive off the damn diving board.

The next day, I watched the clock on the wall in my eleven o'clock study hour in the library, as the hour and minute hands inched their way straight up to twelve. Lots of other boys and girls and teachers also were watching the clock in great anticipation. I wondered if they also had reasons why they wouldn't mind if the world did come to an end at noon.

The hands on the library clock both moved straight up to twelve. The building didn't shake and the only sound was the bell ringing. A minute past noon, nothing happened.

I got up and started for the cafeteria. After lunch, I was going to have to dive off the diving board after all.

Somehow, I did it, but sure didn't like it.

About a week later, we had our last gym class before graduation. All of us guys were in our white gym shorts and tee shirts, playing a last game of basketball. When the gym teacher blew the whistle and our last class ended, it started...

The tradition at Wells High School was that after the last gym class before gradation, senior boys tore each other's gym clothes off. Most of the guys got their shorts and shirts torn off them right away, but I was still shy.
I didn't want mine torn off, so I ran. I knew that would get the guys after me even more, but couldn't help it.

Running down the stairs from the gym to the shower room, half a dozen guys chased me. They almost cornered me against some wall lockers, but I got away and ran into the shower. That's where I got it. Three guys tore my shorts and shirt off me, then left the shower waving the shreds of them over their heads.

I realized I'd survived that, too, as I had dived off the diving board. Grudgingly, I had to admit to myself... Both experiences had been kind of fun and made me feel better about myself.

Four years had passed quickly and it was late spring, 1948. A few days before graduation, I was returning to class one day after going home for lunch. A little boy was playing on his front porch and, while passing him, I waved and said, "Hello."

The boy got up excitedly and called to his mother inside the house:

"Mommy, that man said hello to me!"

Somehow, I believed him. I wasn't a boy anymore.

Chapter Eighteen

I'll get by, as long as I have you

No colleges or corporations big or small sent recruiters to the graduating class of 1948 at Wells High school. Years later I learned only a few of my classmates went on to college. Most of the class of several hundred planned to look for jobs right after graduation.

I certainly had no plans for college so I too began looking for a job. Johnny's brother-in-law worked on the assembly line at Motorola on the West Side, making one of the new electronic wonders people were starting to buy -- television sets. He said they were hiring, so I went there.

After I filled out a job application, a man in the personnel department said I could start that morning and he would show me where I would be working.

Alice had nothing on me, my first morning in Work Wonderland. In the first big room we entered in the factory, I saw some people on an assembly line doing something to some radios.

I pictured myself doing the same thing and thought that would be okay, so long as I got paid. But the man from personnel walked right through that department and into another, and I followed. In the next big room, more people were doing something to some television sets. I tried picturing myself doing that work and thought it would be okay, too. But the personnel man walked right through that department, too, and again I followed.

This kept on until I thought the factory would run out of rooms or departments. My feet were getting tired of walking through them. My head also was getting tired as I pictured myself working in each department we entered. After passing through another four or five rooms, I no longer saw people working on radios or television sets. They were working on everything but them.

Finally, we reached what Christopher Columbus might have thought was the end of the world. It was another big room, this one with cement floor and walls like a garage, and men in overalls were doing something to bus seats.

"We'll start you in here," the personnel man said. "You'll be tearing down old bus seats and rebuilding them."

Bus seats? At an electronics company that makes radios and television sets? I couldn't figure that out, but went along with it and watched the rest of the day while a man unbuilt a bus seat, then rebuilt it with every tool imaginable. I tried picturing myself doing what he was doing to a bus seat, but couldn't quite visualize it.

When five o'clock neared, the foreman came up to me and asked how I spelled my last name. I asked why and he said, "So it can be engraved on your tool wagon."

Tool wagon? I looked around the shop and saw that each worker had his own tool chest standing about waist high, with wheels on it. The rolling tool boxes held a full assortment of gadgets from wrenches and crowbars to drills and soldering equipment. I'd never seen so many tools in my life and didn't know what half of them were for.

I told the foreman how my name was spelled but couldn't imagine myself ever working with or using all those tools.

That night I told my mother and father about my first day on the job. When I told Dad about all the tools and the tool wagon I'd be working with the next morning, he shook his head.

I could guess why. He had been an expert auto mechanic and could tear down a car, engine and all, and rebuild it. But he had never shown me how to do anything more technical than repair a worn lamp cord.

"It's nothing against you," Dad told me, "but you've never learned to use drills and electric saws and all the rest of those tools. You might cut your arm off."

I couldn't have agreed more.

Dad asked Mom to call Motorola the next morning and tell them I wasn't coming back. She agreed.

I felt a great sense of relief that I wasn't going to cut an arm off while tearing down a bus seat.

Mom had taken my side before, but it was only the second time Dad had sided with me that I could remember. The only other time was when I made the candied pork chops.

Before I could find a new job, we moved. Mom must have had the seven year itch. We had lived in the Marshfield Avenue flat that long and since both Mary and I had by then graduated from high school, Mom wanted to move again.

For the first time, we moved into a building that was owned by someone we knew. Mom's parents had come to this country from Austria on the same boat with some friends from their village. Their daughter Ida grew up, married, and she and her husband owned a small two-story house on Sedgwick Street on the near Northwest Side in Old Town. We moved into the apartment on the second floor and had fun spoiling their little boy and girl, Louie and Elizabeth, whom everyone called "Schatzie," which is German for "sweetheart."

It was a balloon-frame house, the type that had been popular in the city at the time of the great Chicago Fire of 1871. Most of them had been destroyed in the fire but afterwards more were rebuilt from the ashes.

Ours was a small two-bedroom apartment and there were three of us to live there, so Mom and Dad had one bedroom, Sis had the other, and I slept on a roll-away cot in the living room. Every evening I rolled it out of a closet and set it up, slept on it, and in the morning rolled it back into the closet.

Many's a morning, around three o'clock, I heard foot-steps on the back stairs and woke up. It was Dad, coming home from a late shift driving the Lake Street elevated trains from the far West Side of the city to the Loop.

Mom got up and they sat together at the kitchen table and drank coffee and talked softly. I was always in that netherworld, halfway between being asleep and being awake, and never heard what they said. I figured they were talking things over again, about his gambling and drinking and not being dependable about bringing home his pay.

Even though I could sense they were having serious talks and things weren't going well, just the sound of their soft voices was kind of comforting to me. I woke up for just a few minutes, then went back to sleep with a feeling that things might not be perfect, but they were still all right.

Sis and I liked living there and loved the kids. Even when Schatzie came upstairs to our back porch and hugged her cat so strong, it squealed and jumped out of her arms. Then Louie scooped the cat up and threw it over our railing. It was a high second floor and that cat must have used up ten times its nine lives because no matter how it got flung off the porch, it always landed on its feet and scampered away.

While we lived on Sedgwick and I still didn't have a new job, a friend from high school telephoned and said I ought to go work where he and some of our other schoolmates were working. The U.S. Treasury Department was operating a microfilm department at the Merchandise Mart near downtown, filming millions of war bond stubs so they would take up less room on microfilm reels than they did in file cabinets in warehouses.

I went to work there and though the job didn't have a future, the pay was okay. The only thing was, after about a week, I was starting to go nuts watching millions of war bond stubs moving up a small movie screen on my desk one-by-one, making sure they had been filmed clearly. Staring at the slow-moving procession of stubs for eight hours a day began to be tiring. Today people think nothing of watching line-after-line of data move up their computer screens and it doesn't drive them batty. Or does it?

The Treasury job gave me time to think what I might do with the rest of my life. Some of the workers about my age were college students, just working there for the summer. They were going back to school in the fall and some told me I ought to start college. But that took money, and that was still in short supply in my bank account.

That was the year Citation made horse-racing history. I wouldn't have paid any attention to the horse winning 25 out of 27 races including the Kentucky Derby, the Preakness, and the Belmont Stakes except I kept hearing Dad and Mom talking about it. They said that at the Pimlico Special, Citation galloped alone around the track. No other horse was regarded its equal.

It wasn't until then that I realized Dad didn't only gamble by playing poker. He played the horses, too. But since he rarely went to the two race tracks in Chicago's western suburbs, Arlington Park in Maywood and Hawthorne in Cicero, he placed his bets on the nags at bookie parlors. He seemed to have the same luck playing the horses as he did playing poker, so it didn't matter much to me at the time.

The summer we lived on Sedgwick a surprise visitor came for a weekend. Dad's old pal from Anderson, Jack Lavergne, the boxer, had gotten married, had a son, and died a few years later. The son, Jack Jr., came to visit and turned out to be a tall, dark-haired, handsome boy my same age who talked kind of intellectually about art and classical music, but wasn't interested in much else.

He said he played both the piano and pipe organ back home and wanted to play for me, but we didn't have either. There wasn't even a harmonica in the house. If I wanted to make music, I'd play a kazoo or put a sheet of Dad's roll-your-own cigarette paper over a comb, put my lips to it, and hum a tune. That wasn't exactly what Jack had in mind for a concert of maybe Beethoven or Bach.

I liked Jack except for a word he kept using all the time, if he disapproved of or didn't like something. He would wrinkle his nose and express his displeasure by saying "Foo-goo." I figured I knew what it stood for, and that didn't bother me. But I'd rather have heard him say the F word ninety times a day than "Foo-goo."

Mom told me, "He thinks the sun rises and sets on you." I thought that was something, because I never thought I made that much impression on anyone.

Jack stayed a weekend and, after returning to Anderson, wrote me. He suggested that since I was interested in writing and he was a musician, we should collaborate on a new grand opera. He would compose the music and I would write the libretto.

I had never seen an opera. I had only seen one movie about that grand form of theater, the Marx Brothers in "A Night at the Opera." That couldn't have been what Jack had in mind for our masterpiece.

About all I knew of opera was that some fat lady wearing horns on her head stood on the stage and sang like a bull moose in heat. But I put my imagination to work and wrote the first scene of Act One of "Daughter of Egypt." My plot may have been inspired by reading about "Aida." In my opera, an Egyptian king was going to boil his daughter's slave-boyfriend in oil if the young man didn't stop trying to take her from a prince the king had in mind for her.

We moved again before I could write any more and I didn't tell Jack where we went. I don't think I did that on purpose. Time just sort of passed and I forgot about our collaboration.

Come to think of it, I don't recall Jack ever writing back with his opinion of the first scene which I wrote and sent him. In any case, to my knowledge, the opera has never been staged.

The autumn of 1948, a new form of entertainment caught my interest, as it had just about everyone else in the country.

My mother and sister were still working as telephone operators for Ma Bell then. One pay day, Sis bought our first television set. It had a small six-inch screen that didn't show a very big picture, but I never got tired of watching the tube.

Some manufacturer came out with a gadget that could make a television picture look bigger, and we bought it. It was a large, heavy magnifying lens that hooked over the back of the TV set and hung over the front of the screen. If you looked straight-on at the screen, it enlarged the picture to about twice its size.

The drawback was, only the person seeing the screen head-on saw the enlarged picture clearly at all. Everyone else saw a blurred curved picture. Still, we left it on and most of the time half of us saw half a small picture and half a larger one.

The years 1948 and 1949 were the heydays of the first big comedian of television, "Uncle Miltie," Milton Berle, and Arthur Godfrey and his talent show. The local Chicago television stars were Dave Garroway and Kookla, Pauline, and Ollie.

In the early years of television, there wasn't that much on. Even the three networks sometimes shared the same program. If you tuned to one station and a woman was singing, then switched to another channel, the same woman would be singing the same song. And they used to call these "variety" shows!

Most of the movies shown on television back then were either real old or had been the second feature on a theater program from about ten years before. On Friday nights a used car dealer sponsored a movie that might not be twenty years old but only about five.

For this "First Time on Television" blockbuster with maybe Claire Trevor or William Gargan, good actors but not exactly superstars, you had to sit through about a twenty-minute commercial before the movie began, watching the car dealer, "Friendly Bob" Something, show about a dozen cars on his lot. Then in the middle of the movie there would be another commercial in which "Friendly Bob" showed about *three* dozen cars.

During this seemingly endless intermission, you could take a bath, wash the car, go grocery shopping or, if you had a dog, walk it a couple of miles before the second half of the movie came on. By then, you'd forgotten what the first half was about or who was in the picture.

Chicago television was experimenting with pay television in 1949. If people in one part of the city paid a few dollars a week, a signal was unscrambled so they could watch a newer movie. We weren't in the test area so even if we paid, we couldn't unscramble the picture. It would roll and jiggle, but the sound was okay.

Some amateur electronics geniuses claimed that if a television set was placed in front of a refrigerator with its door open, the picture would unscramble. Others claimed the picture would be okay if an electric fan blew at the screen.

We tried both, but nothing improved the picture on that pay channel, yet we watched it every night. Our eyes had to put up with the rolling and jiggling and it was almost impossible to tell Clark Gable from Lana Turner in "Somewhere I'll Find You." But we watched the whole movie and wondered why our eyes burned and the house seemed to be rolling and jiggling.

On Saturday nights there was wrestling and roller derby to watch on TV, for those who didn't go out to a bowling alley or a restaurant to try the new culinary craze, pizza.

I didn't care for wrestling or roller derby and wasn't a very good bowler, so I tried pizza.

The first pizza I ate, I didn't like the looks of it. It looked like the waitress had dropped the order on the floor and just scooped up the cheese and tomatoes and sausage slices and smeared them on top the big, round pie. It didn't even taste that good.

The next time I had pizza it was in a darker, just candle-lit restaurant, and it tasted great. I figured it out that the first restaurant had been brightly-lighted and I had gotten too good a look at what I was eating. After I decided that pizza tasted better than it looked, we got along better.

There was a movie theater a few blocks from our house that showed only imported German and Austrian movies. My father never went with us to the Kino, but some nights my mother and sister and I went there, sometimes with Mom's sister, our Aunt Mary, or Aunt Fanny. She was a friend of my maternal grandmother's who had come over on the boat with her from the "Old Country" years before. Aunt Fanny lived a block away and was nice to us and gave us some of her wonderful home-baked cookies and fruit bread. She was a large, round old woman who looked like Santa Claus without the beard, although she had a little gray mustache like most of the old European ladies in the neighborhood.

We would see a double feature all in German, even though Sis and I didn't understand a word the actors were saying. Actually, you didn't have to know the dialogue to understand most German and Austrian movies imported after World War II. The plots were very predictable. A poor but beautiful peasant girl falls in love with a young, handsome, and rich nobleman. But her brother is a poacher who shoots a deer on the nobleman's estate and the lovers are kept apart until the brother gets drafted into the Nazi army and becomes a war hero.

The movies at the Kino had plenty of yodeling, goats, zithers, and bosoms. I never saw a Polish movie but suspected that since Poland was behind the Iron Curtain, their movies would be like the Russian films I'd seen. In these, strapping young Igor Rostenkovokovoffnovsky meets Ildislav Kamarovinskaya who is also strapping and bosomy besides. They fall in love working side-by-side on the clutch plate assembly line in the tractor division of their village's communal farm factory.

We almost never watched silent movies. Mom liked to talk. But one day when she came home with a loaded grocery bag in both arms, she tripped and fell on the top step of our back stairs. She held onto the groceries but landed on her chin. She broke her jaw and it had to be wired for a month. We kids felt sorry she was in pain, but because she couldn't talk, she couldn't chew us out for anything. It was one of the happiest months of our life.

While most Americans were relaxing after the war and buying houses and lawn mowers, we in Chicago's Old Town were still living in an apartment and my father was still up to his old ways with horses, poker chips, and beer. Though no fun for us, on a global scale our domestic problems weren't very important as the Cold War began, the Soviet Union imposed a blockade of Berlin, and Communists in China took Peking. In June, 1950, U.S. naval and air power was sent to South Korea to hold back the Communists in the North.

That summer, my sister and I hadn't any idea that our mother wanted to move again, after just one year on Sedgwick. Dad told us one night, while Mom was working and he and Sis and I were sitting on the couch watching television. In the middle of "Ted Mack's Original Amateur Hour," while two large cigarette boxes with shapely girls' legs under them were tap-dancing on the screen, Dad got up and turned off the set, then sat down between Mary and me on the couch.

"You don't mind if I turn off the TV, do you?" he asked. "I need to talk to you about something."

Dad had never done that before, and we knew he always liked watching the dancing cigarette box girls on that show. He looked very serious and we sensed that something important was on his mind. "Sure," we said. "It's okay."

"Mom wants us to move again," Dad said. "That's okay. But she's been looking at apartments back in the old neighborhood, around Marshfield. Promise me, will you both?"

Sis and I wondered what he had on his mind. He looked so troubled. What did he want us to promise him?

"Promise you won't let us move back there?" he asked.

It hadn't been such a bad neighborhood, I thought. I wouldn't mind moving back to Marshfield. But for some reason, Dad was dead set against it.

"Never go back," Dad said to us. "Always go ahead. Go forward into something. Never go back into anything that was. When I think we might go back where we'd been, I could cry *blood.*"

That was a pretty strong image. We had never heard him say that before.

Sis and I thought we understood. Dad meant never go backward into the past that had been troubled and a failure. Always go *forward,* into a future that had hope of being better. To go back to an old neighborhood meant to admit defeat. It meant going back where there would be no hope.

There weren't tears in Dad's eyes, but a desperate look.

"Promise, you won't let Mom take us back anywhere?" he pleaded.

Sis and I both began to tremble. It had been the most serious talk we ever had with our father or anyone. We could see how much it meant to him. He hadn't been drinking. We had never seen him so serious. We promised.

Chapter Nineteen

Sunrise, sunset. Sunrise, sunset,
Swiftly flow the days

Since they first married, my mother and father always had a dream. It was their ambition to move out of Chicago and live in a suburb by the time they celebrated their twenty-fifth wedding anniversary.

We were living on Sedgwick Street in 1950 and their anniversary was coming up in less than two years. My brother helped make their dream come true.

A friend of Johnny's from the Navy lived in Cicero, the first suburb Southwest of Chicago. His parents owned a house there and lived on the second floor. The first floor was for rent and we moved into it.

Ironically, the house we moved to in Cicero was just one block west of Chicago, west of Cermak Road on 23rd Place. But it didn't matter to my father. He made it. He moved to a suburb before his silver wedding anniversary.

I always thought rich people lived in suburbs, because Dad and Mom seemed to think that. When we first moved to one, I felt we had finally joined the rich people. It wasn't until the routine settled in and I got to know the suburb better that I came to realize a suburb, or at least Cicero, wasn't much different from Chicago or any of the neighbor-hoods we'd lived in. There were poor people, people with money and nice homes and cars, and there were people like us, somewhere in between. Every suburb has to have poor people and working-class people like us. Somebody's got to empty the garbage.

It was only the second time we lived in an actual house, but the first time we lived on the first floor. I felt like socially we were coming up in the world, even though physically we were coming down.

The landlord and his wife were very nice to us but it was a puzzle to me why he kept one bedroom in their upstairs apartment full of cases of beer. It was like a regular liquor store in that room. Had he taken advantage of a good sale or was he afraid some night he might have a thirst and run out?

But I guess, again, to each his own.

Dad really liked living in Cicero. He wanted to live in a suburb, but it also may have been because there were so many taverns only a block away on Cermak Road. Also, there was a bookie joint across from the Western Electric plant a block away on Cicero Avenue. It wasn't that he drank that much more, it was just that he was still coming home some weeks without his pay envelope.

One thing he did a lot of in Cicero was no problem. He liked going to a nearby stadium one night a week when he wasn't working and watch professional women's softball games. He rooted for them as he had for Cubs' stars Gabby Hartnett, Phil Cavaretta, and Hank Sauer and the Sox's Luke Appling and Minnie Minoso.

We went to Mass every Sunday, as we always did when the family was all together. One morning while we were sitting in the church waiting for service to begin, Dad bolted out of his seat. He began running up the main aisle to the altar. Some altar boys were lighting the candles, and we wondered why Dad was running to them so excitedly.

Moments before Dad reached one of the acolytes, the boy's waist-length lace cassock caught fire. Dad took off his suit coat and smothered the flames before they could spread or burn the boy.

Dad explained to us, afterward. He'd been kneeling in our pew and praying while watching the altar boys start to light the candles on the altar. He saw that one of them was approaching a row of lighted votive candles. He had a premonition that the boy would lean too far forward and his cassock would catch fire. Dad's sixth sense may have saved the boy's life and the church from burning down.

On the lighter side, we had a parakeet back then, in a cage in the kitchen, a blue bird named Skipper. We all taught it to speak and before long, it began chirping its name and "Skipper's a pretty boy."

Mom began teaching him all our names and some other things. One night while she was baking and Dad was napping in the bedroom just off the kitchen, Skipper chirped, "Quiet, Grandma. Grandpa's sleeping!"

For about a month after Thanksgiving, we tried teaching the bird to say "Merry Christmas." We thought it would take that long for it to learn the words, in time to greet us for the holiday. But Skipper just wouldn't say the words. Finally we gave up and instead began trying to teach him to say "Happy Birthday, Mary," for my sister's birthday in January.

Dad, Mom, Sis and I were going to Midnight Mass that Christmas Eve. Just as we opened the kitchen door to leave, Skipper chirped, "Happy Birthday, Mary Christmas!"

I didn't know at the time, but it was going to be a very good year for me.

We had a car then, a used Nash, and some Sundays we drove into the city to visit Grandpa at the old house on Peoria Street. On one visit, early in 1951, I was introduced to an aunt who was new to the family. One of Dad's younger brothers, Ray, who was built and looked like him, tall and strong, had married a college English teacher.

Aunt Margaret was a studious-looking woman of medium frame who had reddish hair and wore glasses. She sat on the radiator cover with me in the living room at Grandpa's that Sunday and asked what I was working at. I had left the Treasury Department and was working in the garage at the *Chicago Tribune*, handing out carburetors, generators, and other parts to the truck drivers who delivered bundles of the papers to newsstands and stores around the city.

I told her I'd answered an ad for a copy boy's job there, but a man in personnel told me it had been filled. When he saw on my application that I had worked at the Treasury Department in microphotography, he said he'd like to hire me to work in the newspaper's microfilm department which they were going to start in a couple of years. The man in personnel wanted to hire me right then and put me in some-thing temporary until the microfilm department opened.

"What did you like to do least in high school?" the man asked.

I didn't hesitate a second. "Math," I replied.

"How would you like to work in our accounting department?" he asked.

Heck, I didn't know. "That'd be fine."

I figured maybe if I got a job on the newspaper, doing anything, one day I'd finally realize my big ambition to become a newspaper reporter there.

When the accounting department learned how bad I was at using the adding machine, I was transferred to the garage, to hand out the truck parts.

After I described my career at the *Tribune*, Aunt Margaret asked, "Have you thought of going to college?"

"College? That's just for rich kids."

"Did you know you can go for two years to Navy Pier Illinois, where I teach English, for only forty dollars a semester?" she asked.

After I learned from her that there was a two-year branch of the University of Illinois in Chicago at Navy Pier, I wanted to go. The next night I asked Mom and Dad and Sis if I could quit work in the *Tribune* garage and go to Navy Pier, to get at least two years of college. They were all for it.

My mother went with me on the elevated the morning I was to register at Navy Pier. As the train crossed the Chicago River and entered the Loop, I told her, "I'm really glad about going to college. Now I won't be bored anymore."

I'd been bored ever since graduating from high school, and had taken some night courses in writing at a Loop college. But starting college full-time was the most exciting thing that had ever happened to me.

Before classes began, Dad took me on a shopping trip to buy me a couple of sport coats to wear at college. He took me to Maxwell Street on the near Southwest Side of the city, a shopping district known for the best bargains in town. It was several blocks of stores side-by-side selling just about everything at discount prices, and the salesmen were the most persistent anywhere. Some if not most of the merchandise was believed to be hot, stolen from somewhere else and resold there.

It was funny because before I had started high school, Dad had taken me to Maxwell Street and bought me a sport coat. I wore it for four years until it wore out. Now he took me back there to shop for sport coats for college.

Despite the seedy look of Maxwell Street, the two sport coats Dad bought me were very good-looking, a brown plaid and a blue herringbone. I never had any sport coats last me as long as those.

Navy Pier was a strange place to have a college. It was a long narrow building that extended a mile out into Lake Michigan at the foot of Chicago Avenue. When I was a boy, we had gone there to spend a summer day at a carnival, took a boat ride, or went fishing off the pier. During World War II, Navy Pier became a base for training sailors. After the war, it became a two-year city college in order to accommodate many returning servicemen who wanted to take advantage of the G.I. bill and get at least a couple of years of a college education.

I went to college at Navy Pier by day and studied at home by night, meeting new friends and for the first time, dating regularly. The girl was one of the church friends of my best new friend at college, Harry. She seemed to want to get serious but I had too much on my mind for that. I had two years of college ahead of me and was hoping to find some way of going on afterward. I wanted to complete the other two so I could have a college degree and maybe get back on at the *Tribune* as a reporter.

Uncle Ray and Aunt Margaret, who had become Aunt Maggie to me by then, had an apartment near Navy Pier. Every Friday afternoon after our last classes, I went to the English department and she was ready to leave. We walked a few blocks to the apartment and played canasta and drank beer until Ray got home from work as a menswear salesman. He laughed, started dinner for us, and then got in the game. After dinner, we played three-handed canasta until about midnight.

They drove me all the way home to Cicero afterward. They wouldn't come in, just dropped me off at the front door, turned around, and drove all the way back to their place. It was well over an hour each way, so they were lucky if they got back home by two in the morning.

Those canasta Fridays became a very enjoyable, anticipated routine for the three of us. In a way, they seemed to be an extension of the weekend poker games at Grandma's.

Dad was glad my aunt and uncle and I were together so often but I sensed Mom was a little jealous. She needn't have been. I appreciated Aunt Maggie being instrumental in my going to college, but had Mom and Dad and Sis to thank for my being able to go. And I loved both Mom and Aunt Maggie, just in different ways.

The Korean war was still on in 1951. I picked up the newspaper one day and an article on the front page drew my attention. It was an open letter from a girl in Chicago asking someone to explain to her why her fiancée had been sent to Korea and had just gotten killed there.

I read the letter without knowing, until the very end of her letter, that her fiancée had been the good-looking, curly-haired teenager I'd worked with in Wieboldt's shipping room during high school. The All-American boy who always pretended he was shooting baskets.

The letter-writer's fiancée had been my first really great friend, Freddie Hartzell. He had been killed just a short time before the truce came in Korea that November. Like his fiancée, I wondered too, as I do now... Why did the boy with more life in him than anyone I had ever known have to die so tragically, so far from home, and so young?

The classrooms at Navy Pier were often under water in springtime when the level of the lake rose. In winter, the wind blew so hard over the water that it made a sheet of ice out front of the entrance. One morning going in, a gale wind began blowing a girl from one of my classes toward the frozen lake just beside the entrance. The wind tore her raincoat right off and she began sliding toward the icy water. I reached out and grabbed her by one hand and held onto an awning post with the other until I could pull her back to safety.

The following May, Mom and Dad celebrated their twenty-fifth wedding anniversary and the whole family came to the house for the party. The only thing that Dad could have enjoyed more happened soon after. Johnny's wife gave birth to a baby girl. Mom and Dad were grandparents, Sis became an aunt, and I an uncle.

I was involved with a little one, too. No, not in the way you might think. For an exam in biology our class had to dissect a rat. We could take our specimen home on a Friday and study it over the weekend, bringing it back on Monday for the test. Aunt Maggie invited me to canasta and dinner again that Friday so I asked if I could bring a friend.

She was always hoping I'd bring a girlfriend, but I disappointed her by saying I'd like to bring my new friend, Mickey.

"Sure, bring him along," she said.

I had to run some errands before dinner so we didn't walk to her place that day. After Uncle Ray had gotten home from work, I arrived and rang their apartment bell.

"Where's Mickey?" Aunt Maggie asked, not seeing anyone with me at the door.

I held up a small metal fishing tackle box I'd brought along and said, "He's in here."

I explained about my yellowed friend soaking in formaldehyde inside the tackle box and Aunt Maggie pointed to the kitchen door. I took the box fast as I could through the apartment and out the back door, setting my specimen down on the porch. It was a cold night, but in Mickey's condition, he wouldn't mind being there.

I passed biology, but failed hygiene. It wasn't because I hadn't learned from my sister about underarm deodorant, or the things the instructor added to the list of what gentlemen should and should not do to be clean of body and mind. It was because during the final, when the instructor left the classroom for a few minutes, half the students got out of their seats and began exchanging answers to the final exam.

Upon his return, the instructor said everyone who had been out of his seat during the exam would get an "F" and fail the course. I had been out of my seat, so I failed and had to take hygiene over again that spring. Failing hygiene became a blight on my character I could never erase.

I credit Aunt Maggie with saving me from flunking biology. I was still having trouble with the sex life of frogs and wasn't much better dissecting a rat, but my real problem was multiple-choice exams. I could get an A in just about any written exam, but picking out a right answer from a list of four or five choices stumped me.

After coming out of the final exam in biology, a bunch of us in class waited in the hall for the instructor to grade our tests because he said he would do it fast. After we waited about an hour, he gave out with the bad news. About a fourth of the class failed.

I looked at my grade and saw, to my relief, that I hadn't failed but had gotten a "D."

"You lucky son of a gun, you passed!" one of my failing classmates told me.

The instructor took me aside and said, "I don't know how you did it. If there were five choices of answer and four of them were right, you picked the wrong one!"

That was how it was with me and multiple-choice.

Later I learned how I passed the course. Aunt Maggie had warned the instructor before the final,

"If you flunk my nephew, I'll call the F.B.I. and tell them the whole biology department is full of Commies!"

Aunt Maggie, like many people in the early 1950s, suspected that Soviet Communists had infiltrated higher education in America. I didn't know about that and never thought I saw a Communist at Navy Pier, but was glad she felt that way. If she hadn't, I might still be taking biology and dissecting rats.

Aunt Maggie also was the reason I dropped out of working on the college newspaper and turned instead to politics. She was a great teacher and had many friends among the students and faculty, but because she was so good she also had some jealous enemies. I began to find this influencing my promotion or lack of it on the student newspaper, so after just my first quarter, I quit, even though my major was pre-journalism.

My friend Harry was president of a student organization called the Quad Council which was working hard to influence legislators into expanding the then two-year University of Illinois on Navy Pier into a full four-year school. I left the newspaper and joined him in that crusade, becoming vice-president of the council.

One day we were going to hold a noon rally in the auditorium, to drum up more student and faculty enthusiasm for a four-year university in Chicago, and invited reporters from the then-four daily newspapers in the city. Shortly before noon I saw so few students in the auditorium, I went into the cafeteria and got up on a table. I shouted to the students to take their lunches into the auditorium and show strong student support for the four-year school. It roused only a few of the lunchers to move to the rally.

Afterward, Aunt Maggie said she had seen me and was proud of what I did. Cousin Tom who started at Navy Pier a year after me had been watching as I urged the lunch crowd to move to the rally, and he cringed. He couldn't believe his normally quiet cousin had the nerve to get up on a table and shout the way I had. Neither had I!

Still, attendance at the rally was disappointing. Afterward, when a reporter for one of the daily papers asked if I thought it was successful, I told him how I felt:

"I was very disappointed more students and faculty didn't turn out for the rally. If we're going to influence legislators to vote for a four-year university in Chicago, we have to show we want it!"

My quote to the press was viscerally true, but when the newspaper came out, I realized that politically it had been a mistake. The reporter quoted me exactly and it merely served to demonstrate to the politicians opposed to the expense of a four-year university in the city that there wasn't enough interest in the plan, even from present students and faculty.

I realized I had not played winning politics that day. I should have told the reporter something like,

"It was a great turn-out. More than we expected. It just goes to show how badly a four-year school is wanted."

I felt bad about how I had blown the interview. I felt about worse than I ever had in my life. I felt stupid.

When I talked about it to my German teacher, Frau Teichmann, who favored the four-year school, she was kind enough to tell me,

"Don't worry about today's mistakes. Just learn from them. Next time, you'll think a step ahead when you talk to a newspaper reporter or anyone else. Tell them what you want them to print. That's politics."

It was one of the best lessons I ever learned, about how to be a good politician and also how to be a good reporter.

If I was learning in those areas, I still wasn't much of a jock. As an elective in gym one semester I took wrestling. I stood about six foot two inches tall and weighed about 145 pounds, not exactly competition for Moose Cholock.

For the final exam, the instructor scratched his head while trying to match the class up in pairs. He had just about all the guys paired off except me and looked stumped for a partner my size.

Finally, he saw only one solution. He matched the tallest, thinnest guy, me, with the biggest and fattest.

"It's just to demonstrate you know the take-downs and holds," the instructor told me. "Don't worry about winning."

That was the least of my worries. When my opponent, about a thousand pounds of flab, tossed me onto my back and buried my face in his stomach I only worried about breathing.

I was better at golf, but not much, though I liked it a lot more than any other sport I'd tried. That spring after my first year in college, I went golfing at Chicago area courses with Johnny some Saturdays and also at times with Mom and Dad and Sis.

Mary was then twenty-three, still working for Ma Bell but in one of the Loop offices by then and no longer an operator but in charge of "switchboard mortality." If a business customer closed an office, Sis arranged that their telephone switchboard would be taken away. She was dating but hadn't yet found anyone who really rang her bell. Neither had I.

One Saturday golfing with my sister we were on a fairway when I saw her hit a good long five-iron shot. It lofted high and was going to come down in the middle of the fairway and in a good lie to the green. Before I could call out to her how good her shot was, I saw she was running like crazy in the direction her ball was flying. She was very agitated about something.

I wondered why she was so upset until I saw it. A gopher was racing across the fairway from left to right as Mary's ball was starting its downward arc. It didn't require expertise in geometry to see that her ball was in danger of hitting the gopher.

At first I thought she was afraid her ball would hurt the gopher. Then I realized what was upsetting her so much. She was afraid that if her ball hit the gopher, the ball wouldn't get any extra roll toward the green.

Was this my sweet, gentle sister who was normally kind to animals, I wondered, or some golf fiend?

Swinging her five-iron over her head and hollering "Get away from my ball!" Sis ran toward the gopher, meaning to bean it if she had to.

Fortunately for the gopher, it found refuge in a hole just before Mary's ball could hit it. Her ball landed on the turf and tragedy was averted. Did it get much roll? Not that I noticed.

My mother and father loved playing golf together on the rare times they joined Johnny or Mary and me. Mom always hit her ball just a short distance but straight as an arrow. Dad hit his a lot farther but usually hooked or sliced to one side or the other off the fairway and landed in the rough. By the time he took his next shot, he was lucky to get his ball back where Mom had hit hers so short but with such accidental precision.

Dad always kept score for him and Mom on the same card. When they putted out, he always asked her what her score was first.

"It took me thirteen on that hole," she would lament.

"It only took me ten," Dad would say, then marked the score card.

It didn't seem to occur to Mom that Dad may have been playing with the numbers by asking her score first. We didn't want to spoil it for Dad so we never suggested the possibility. But maybe my mother knew what my father's trick was all the time. She just let him get away with it.

One afternoon while my father and I were golfing, he hit a long, straight ball that landed him on a slight hill to the left of the fairway, only about twenty-five yards from the green. As I saw him get ready for his approach shot, he was about to swing with a three wood. That might not have lifted the ball out of the grass on the hill or would have hit the ball too far, so I called to him,

"Try a seven iron, Dad!"

He took my advice, the only time I ever remember him doing that. He put his wood back in the bag and took out his seven iron. Swinging with uncharacteristic professional ease, he hit the ball squarely. It rose from the turf, lofted into the air, then began falling in a beautiful arc toward the green. It landed in about the lower half of the green. We both watched in wonder as the ball, as if guided by providence, rolled into the cup.

Dad had never gotten a birdie before. He danced up and down on top the hill, holding his seven iron triumphantly over his head. I had never seen my father happier.

He looked as if he knew: he finally got a break.

Chapter Twenty

Show me the way to go home,
I'm tired and I want to go to bed

My sister began having fun at her Loop office early in 1952 exchanging wisecracks over the telephone with an installer who also worked on switchboard mortality but worked outside the office, in the field. He liked to do a lot of innocent kidding and Sis picked up on it and kept it going. He only told her his first name, which was John.

This went on daily for several months, neither Mary nor the installer expecting anything romantic to come of it. Then one Saturday she went to a telephone company party and during the course of the evening joined a small group of people who were talking and laughing together. Someone introduced Mary to one of the young men in the group and he looked at her with special interest.

"Are you Mary?" he asked.

"Are you John?" she asked.

They began dating and a few months later, my sister announced the good news: She and John were engaged.

"Aw," I replied, "then we won't be able to go to the show anymore."

I couldn't help the initial reaction I had to her engagement, but a moment later hugged her and told her how happy I was for her.

It made me realize that meeting a girl I might fall in love with and ask to marry me might not be as difficult as I'd thought. Mary and John had met in a very simple, casual way. Their paths, it seemed, had been destined to cross.

Like my cousin Betty from Springfield who had so regularly and faithfully visited the gorilla Bushman until he died and left a big hole in so many people's hearts. About a year later, while carrying groceries through a hotel lobby in Springfield, Betty tripped over a young man's feet sprawled out in front of him as he slouched in a chair reading a newspaper. He picked up her groceries, then her, and within a year they were married.

It gave me renewed hope that it could happen to me.

Not long after my sister's engagement, during winter quarter at Navy Pier, she and Mom were both at work while my father and I were at home together in the kitchen. The radio was playing soft music and Dad was at the table reading an early edition of the next morning's paper while I was ironing a shirt for school the next day.

Somehow, Dad and I got to talking. I couldn't remember just the two of us talking before as we did that evening. It was easy and relaxed and man-to-man and it felt very good.

After a while, the conversation led to Dad telling about another dream or ambition he had, besides the one he'd had about moving to a suburb. I never knew he had this second desire.

"Your mother and I hope one day we can move to Wisconsin," he said. "We'd like to buy a place on the outskirts of some small town where there are woods and a lake. I'd have a gas station and repair cars. Your mother would cook and bake and run a little diner next door."

It was the first time I'd ever heard him talk about it. It sounded like a great idea and I told him so.

"I'll work hard at college and get on a newspaper afterward as a reporter," I said. "I'll save my money and help you get the place you want."

Dad and I had an understanding that night, for the first time. We seemed to understand each other. Even more important, we respected each other.

I'd always wanted him to hug me, when I was little. To my knowledge, he never did. We didn't hug that night, nor did we shake hands. There was just a mutual respect and liking between us I'd never thought there would be. It was probably because, for the first time, he seemed to have faith that I'd make something of myself. As for my feelings, I had a new respect for him that made up for all the years I hadn't liked him, for staying away from us so many times and causing Mom such heartache.

A few weeks later, during a cold and rainy March, Dad stayed away once again. He hadn't come home after work and Mom again needed his pay. She worried he had lost it all, on the horses this time since he played them at the bookie parlor more than he played poker.

Two nights later my father came home and was very sick. Mom forgave him right away, as she always did when she saw he needed nursing. She put him to bed and saw he had a high fever.

The fever worried her because Chicago was in the grip of a deadly viral infection that winter. The newspaper death notices which usually only ran about one page had been covering two and three pages. People were dying in near-epidemic numbers from "galloping pneumonia."

Mom called our family doctor and he said it sounded as if Dad needed hospital care. But every hospital in and around the city was full. The doctor tried for hours, but was unable to find a hospital with a spare bed for Dad. The best he could do was order an oxygen tent. It was delivered to our flat in Cicero and put over the top of Dad's bed, to help him breathe.

At about two o'clock the next morning, the doctor called saying he found a bed for Dad at Alexian Brothers' hospital on the near Northwest Side in Chicago. My brother Johnny, who rented an apartment near us in Cicero, came over and drove Mom and Dad to the hospital.

All the hospital beds were taken, so Dad was put on a cot in one of the hallways. The doctor said there was little more that could be done until morning so Johnny drove Mom back home.

The doctor called again at about eight o'clock that morning and asked Mom to come to the hospital. Johnny drove Mom and Mary and me there. When we arrived, we waited in the doctor's office for him to give us a report on Dad.

When the doctor arrived at his office and began telling us about Dad, it puzzled and frightened Mom.

"Doctor," she said. "You sound as if there isn't any hope for him."

The doctor looked surprised and distressed. "Oh, I'm so sorry," he said. "Then you haven't been told? John passed away, shortly after I called you."

It was the unexpected, sudden realization we had lost him. Johnny, Sis, and I got out of our chairs and went to Mom. We all hugged each other and cried.

Dad was waked at a chapel in Cicero. The first of the three nights, while uncles and aunts and others in the family and many friends arrived to pay their respects, someone entered the parlor that I recognized. I ran to him and hugged him. It was a moment or two before I realized it wasn't Dad I was hugging, but his brother Ray. Tall, solidly built and not yet fifty years old, Uncle Ray looked so much like my father.

After the first night of the wake, Mom and Mary slept in Mom's bed. The next morning Sis told me,

"Mom and I heard chains clanging and a strange light began shining in the bedroom. It started as a tiny light, then kept getting bigger and brighter until it filled the entire room."

My mother and sister had felt very sad and lost, until the bright light filled the bedroom. After the light grew dim again and then went away, a great peace and calm came over them. They were sure the light had been Dad's spirit, come to tell them everything was all right and he had at last found peace.

Later, while waiting for the second night of the wake to begin, I asked Mom about Dad. Had he really preferred gambling and drinking and being with his friends rather than with us, especially on our birthdays or at Easter or Christmas?

"Your father didn't like to gamble at all," she told us. "He just kept hoping he could run his pay money up into more, because we always needed money to pay the bills. He loved you children. All three of you. He tried very hard. Too hard. He just didn't have any luck."

If only he had come home after he'd gotten the cold that developed into pneumonia, she told us. Instead he slept in the old Nash and the heater hadn't been working. If he'd have come home earlier, he might have lived.

The priest who came from our church on the last night of the wake asked Mom,

"Was your husband an alderman?"

"No," she said, almost laughing. "Why do you ask that?"

"It's because I've never seen so many mourners before," he replied. "Except for a bishop or a politician. Last week a Mafia don was waked here. He had more mourners than I'd ever seen before, until tonight, for your husband. He must have been a rich man, with that many friends."

Dad had been rich in friends. He made friends all his life. Most of them came to pay their last respects, including many to whom he loaned five or ten dollars each payday over the years. They didn't leave envelopes with the money they owed, but coming to the wake to say good-bye to him meant even more to us.

After the funeral Mass the next morning, the hearse and entire procession of cars with the bereaved drove from the church to the home of the deceased, as is the custom at Polish funerals. The motorcade drove slowly by the house and then turned onto Cicero Avenue to proceed to Resurrection Cemetery in Southwest suburban Justice.

Dad had been the favorite of the family. It was especially hard for his father and brothers and sisters to lose him, and he had been only fifty-one years old.

Sis and Johnny and I were sitting with Mom in a long black limousine just behind the hearse when it made an unexpected stop. Looking out the window, we saw that the hearse had stopped right in front of the high fence and locked gates of Hawthorne Race Track. The hearse seemed to be having engine trouble because the driver kept revving the engine, but it wouldn't turn over. Finally, after several minutes of stalling, the engine started up and the funeral procession began moving again.

When we arrived at the cemetery and got out to gather at the gravesite, everyone talked of the same thing... Why the procession had stopped on the way to the cemetery.

Mom said she knew why the hearse stopped where it had, and it made some laugh, relieving the tension and sorrow of loss. Sis and Johnny and I knew too, and so did probably the rest of the family.

Dad had gone up the alley and over the fence, to have one last beer and place a final bet.

I thought I understood my father, finally. He had always been chasing rainbows. His dreams, like all his schemes, had faded in the air. Some fellows made a winning sometime; he never seemed to make a gain.

But he tried, as best he could. And he had loved us.

So these are the stories I tell when the younger generation asks, "Tell what it was like, when you were a kid?"

The old neighborhoods have changed some, and new immigrants live in the same flats we lived in. Most of the neighborhood movie palaces were torn down or converted into savings and loans. The Biltmore on Division Street near Damen Avenue where Johnny ushered and sneaked my sister and me in after school to see double features later became known as the San Juan. The juke boxes in the Polish taverns along Milwaukee Avenue and German restaurants on North Avenue began playing tangos instead of polkas and waltzes.

Like many other families in Chicago and across America during The Great Depression and World War II, we found ways to survive, even when times seemed hardest. Latinos and other nationalities are looking for the same thing today.

So are young people in neighborhoods everywhere searching for ways to survive in their speeded up lives with the pressures of the sexual revolution with its resultant increase in teen pregnancy, broken families, drugs, and AIDS. If young people today work at surviving as we did, they can make it too. Years from now they can tell the hard times stories of their youth to their grandchildren.

"Sure as there are little green apples," hard times come for us all, one way or another. Sometimes it seems to come every way possible. The thing to remember in those times is to have faith and don't lose your sense of humor, to help survive them.

As one contemporary philosopher puts it, "Trouble always comes in six delicious flavors." But no matter how bad things looked or got for us during the Great Depression or World War II or afterward, Mom the Family Philosopher always said, "It'll all come out in the wash." And it did and still does, when trouble comes calling, through new recessions or Depressions and wars with terrorism. None of all that is new to us, and we survive.

My sister and mother, more than any others, taught me by example how to survive. In the process, the family survived. Not as complete as we would have wanted, but accepting loss is part of enduring. My mother, father, and some favorite aunts and uncles and cousins have died, but my brother and his wife eventually had four children, and my sister and her husband had four more to add to the family roster. The Lord giveth and the Lord taketh away.

There would be more hard times in our family in the years ahead, after that final good-bye to Dad in Justice.

Were the days of my Chicago boyhood "the good old days"? You bet they were!

I wondered, when I was a sophomore at Navy Pier, would I ever fall in love and marry? I asked my godmother, Aunt Mary, how she had known when she was in love and had wanted to marry my future Uncle John.

"I used to go to a grocery store in my neighborhood on the North side," she said. "I began to talk to the butcher and then to like him. One day I knew I was in love with him when I felt like dancing on top his meat counter."

Did it ever happen to me? Did I ever feel like dancing on top of a meat counter? Did I fall in love and marry? As the old Indian tale-spinner said to foreign listeners around a campfire in *The Jungle Book*, "That, Sahib, is another story."

Made in the USA
San Bernardino, CA
03 February 2019